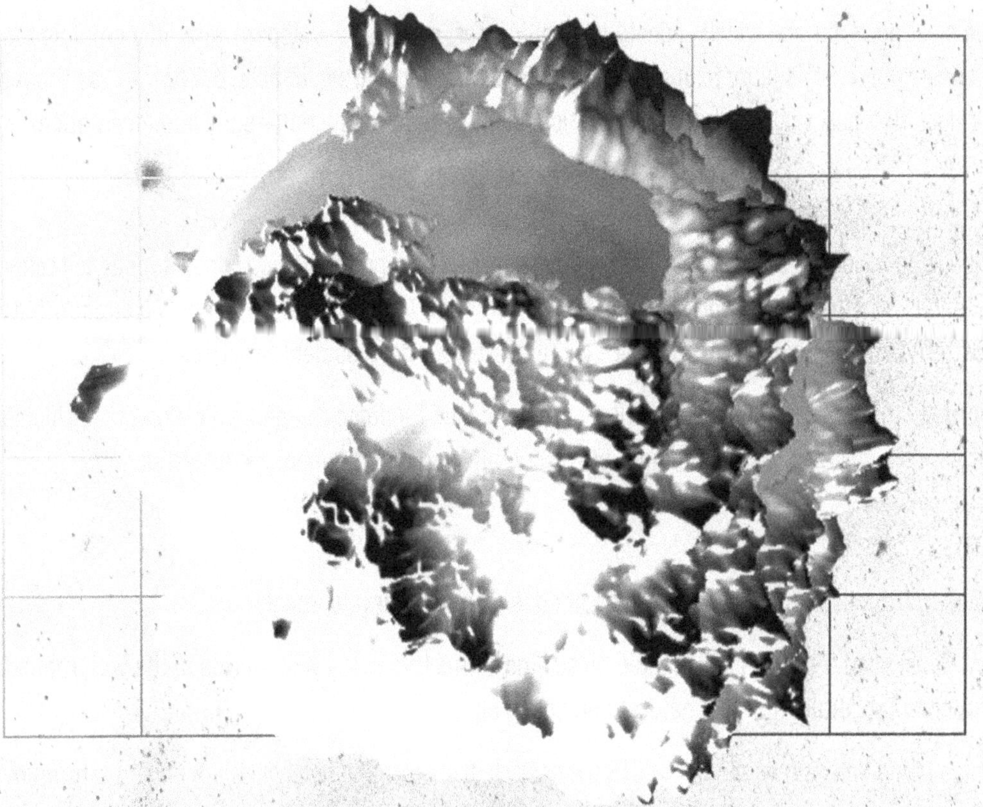

GAME ARCHITECTURE AN ADVANCED APPROACH

LEARN HOW TO MAKE AN | ADVANCED SYSTEMS FOR YOUR GAMES

BY ABDULLAH ASAAD GHALI

Introduction

Modern game development has evolved far beyond simple scripting and basic scene management. Today's games demand sophisticated architectures that can handle complex systems, massive amounts of data, and intricate interactions between multiple components. This book represents a deep dive into the advanced architectural patterns and techniques that separate professional game developers from hobbyists.

Unity, as one of the most powerful and widely-adopted game engines, provides developers with an incredible toolkit. However, with great power comes the responsibility to understand not just what tools are available, but how to use them effectively at scale. This book bridges that gap, taking you from foundational concepts to production-ready implementations.

Who This Book Is For

This advanced guide is designed for Unity developers who have moved beyond the basics and are ready to tackle complex architectural challenges. Whether you're working on indie projects that demand professional polish or contributing to AAA productions, the patterns and techniques covered here will elevate your development practices.

We assume familiarity with C# programming, basic Unity concepts, and fundamental game development principles. This isn't a beginner's tutorial—it's a masterclass in building robust, scalable, and maintainable game systems.

What You'll Learn

Throughout this book, you'll master seven critical areas of advanced Unity development:

Procedural Content Generation through sophisticated noise algorithms that bring your worlds to life with realistic terrain, textures, and environmental details that feel natural and engaging.

Data-Oriented Design using Unity's revolutionary DOTS framework, transforming how you think about performance, memory management, and system architecture for games that can handle thousands of entities simultaneously.

Professional Tool Development by mastering Unity's editor scripting capabilities, creating custom tools that streamline your workflow and empower your entire development team.

Architectural Excellence through proven scripting patterns that make your codebase maintainable, testable, and scalable as your project grows in complexity.

Physics Mastery by diving deep into Unity's physics systems, understanding not just how to use them, but how to optimize and extend them for your specific needs.

Visual Programming through advanced shader development, giving you complete control over your game's visual identity and performance characteristics.

Intelligent Behavior by implementing sophisticated AI systems that create compelling, believable, and engaging non-player characters and game mechanics.

How This Book Is Structured

Each chapter builds upon previous concepts while remaining focused on practical, production-ready solutions. Code examples are drawn from real-world scenarios, and every technique is explained with both the "how" and the "why" to deepen your understanding.

We emphasize best practices, performance considerations, and maintainability throughout. This isn't just about making things work—it's about making them work well, at scale, over time.

Getting the Most From This Book

The concepts in this book are interconnected. While each chapter can serve as a reference, working through them sequentially will give you the deepest understanding of how these systems work together in a cohesive game architecture.

All code examples are production-tested and include performance considerations, memory management strategies, and debugging approaches. We encourage you to experiment with and modify the examples to fit your specific use cases.

Looking Forward

Game development continues to evolve rapidly. The architectural principles and patterns you'll learn here are designed to be timeless—foundational concepts that will serve you well regardless of how tools and technologies change.

As you work through this book, you're not just learning Unity techniques—you're developing the architectural thinking that will make you a more effective developer across any platform or engine.

Let's begin building games that don't just work, but work beautifully.

Chapter I
[NOISE IN VIDEO GAMES]

PerlinNoise :
The perlinNoise function is one of the most well-known and widely used noises. PerlinNoise is a float with two parameters (x, y), so in the declaration we can write [public static float perlinNoise(float x, float y)]. PerlinNoise returns a float value between 0 and 1, but it could be less than zero or greater than one.
PerlinNoise can be described as a 2D texture since it is a pseudo-random pattern of float values generated across a 2D plane. The noise does not have a truly random value at each place but rather consists of "waves" whose values progressively grow and decrease across the pattern.

PerlinNoise Uses :
It has various applications in textures and shaders, but we'll start with a more fascinating one: the usage of perlinNoise in Procedural Generation. Let's begin by generating a grid of cubes in the Unity game engine:
We will start by defining the world size in x and z to a 10 x 10 like this code :

```
private int worldSizeX = 10;
private int worldSizeZ = 10;

private int gridOffset = 2;
```

also we should assign the gameObject which is in our case is a cube and assign the grid offset :

```
public GameObject CubeGameObject;
```

then using a for loop to make sure not to generate outside the world size in the start function :

```
Unity Message | 0 references
void Start()
{
    for(int x = 0; x < worldSizeX; x++)
    {
        for(int z = 0; z < worldSizeZ; z++)
        {
            Vector3 pos = new Vector3(x * gridOffset, 0
                , z * gridOffset);

            GameObject cube = Instantiate(CubeGameObject, pos,
                Quaternion.identity) as GameObject;

            cube.transform.SetParent(this.transform);
        }
    }
}
```

this code make sure that it generates within the world size and start generating until it fills it taking in consideration the margin between them represented as the gridOffset.

Then we create a cube prefab, attach the code to an empty game object, and insert the cube prefab. The result shape should appear like this in play mode:

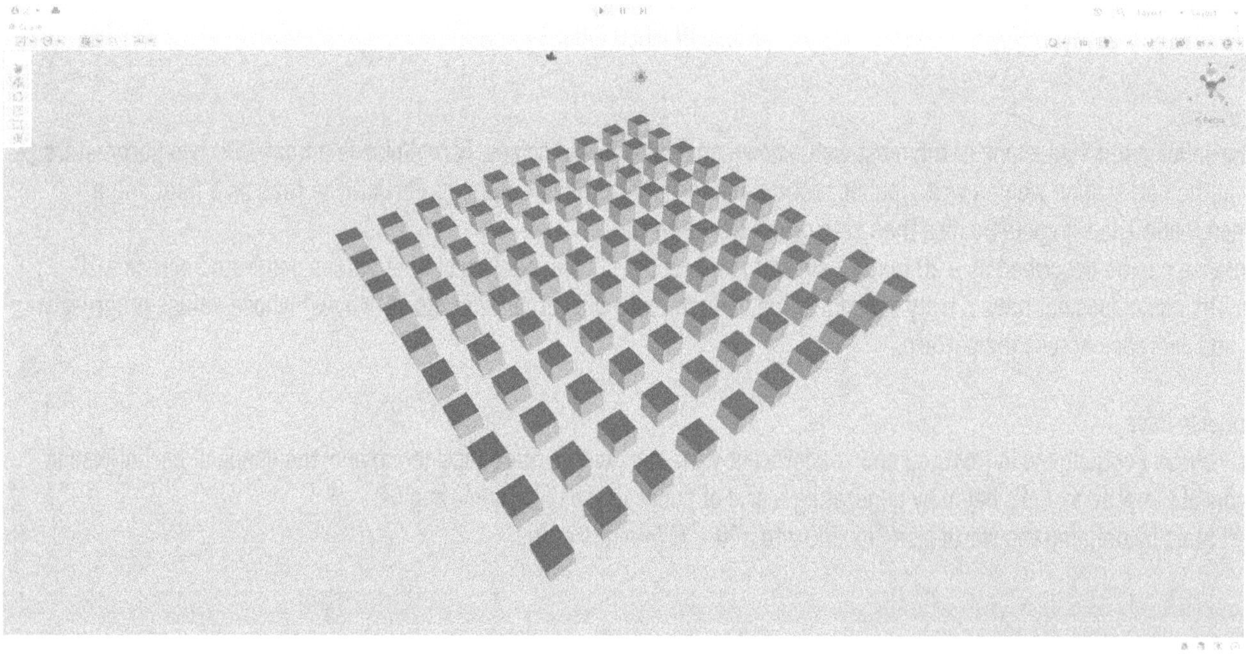

Now to apply the PerlinNoise to the cubes we make a private float function which is called generateNoise it will calculate the NoiseX and NoiseZ by adding x,z to the transform and then dividing by the detail scale, and then we return the mathf function of PerlinNoise as the code below :

```
0 references
private float generateNoise(int x, int z, float detailScale)
{
    float xNoise = (x + this.transform.position.x) / detailScale;
    float zNoise = (z + this.transform.position.y) / detailScale;

    return Mathf.PerlinNoise(xNoise, zNoise);
}
```

Now we have to implement this code inside the Start function :

```
Unity Message | 0 references
void Start()
{
    for(int x = 0; x < worldSizeX; x++)
    {
        for(int z = 0; z < worldSizeZ; z++)
        {
            Vector3 pos = new Vector3(x * gridOffset,
                generateNoise(x,z,8f)
                , z * gridOffset);

            GameObject cube = Instantiate(CubeGameObject, pos,
                Quaternion.identity) as GameObject;

            cube.transform.SetParent(this.transform);
        }
    }
}
```

then we will change some stuff we will make a noise height function and change the gridOffset to a float and make it equal to 1.1 float points :

```
private int NoiseHeight = 3;

private float gridOffset = 1.1f;
```

then we assign the noise height easily by multiplying it with generateNoise function :

```
Vector3 pos = new Vector3(x * gridOffset,
    generateNoise(x,z,8f) * NoiseHeight
    , z * gridOffset);
```

the result in playing mode should be as below :

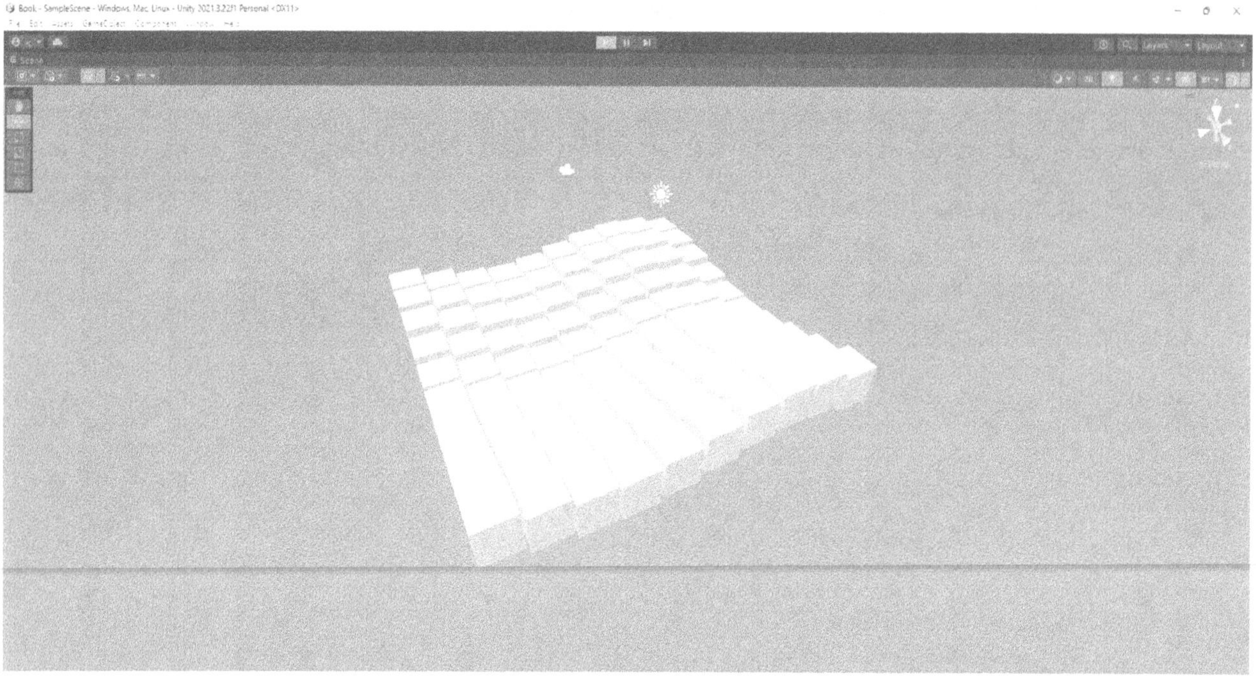

taking another look on noise we could make textures and shaders using noise, so now we will make noise vertex animation we will use perlinNoise on a plane mesh vertices so we can get a wave animation from the noise.
First make a new 3d plane in the hierarchy then make a new c# script called NoiseAnimation, inside the code make 3 floats one for the perlinScale, one for the waveSpeed and one for the waveHeight like the code below :

```
public float perlineScale = 4.5f;
public float waveSpeed = 1f;
public float waveHeight = 2f;
```

now make a private mesh and a new void called AnimateMesh then call it in the update function :

```
private Mesh mesh;

Unity Message | 0 references
void Update()
{
    AnimateMesh();
}

1 reference
void AnimateMesh()
{

}
```

now to animate the mesh first we make sure if there was no mesh to generate a mesh filter, then we make a vector3 array of vertices and make it equals to the mesh vertices, then we make a for loop for the perlinNoise for both x and z as we learned before :

```
1 reference
void AnimateMesh()
{
    if(!mesh)
        mesh = GetComponent<MeshFilter>().mesh;

    Vector3[] vertices = mesh.vertices;

    for (int i = 0; i < vertices.Length; i++)
    {
        float pX = (vertices[i].x * perlineScale) + (Time.timeSinceLevelLoad * waveSpeed);
        float pZ = (vertices[i].z * perlineScale) + (Time.timeSinceLevelLoad * waveSpeed);

        vertices[i].y = (Mathf.PerlinNoise(pX, pZ) - 0.5f) * waveHeight;
    }

    mesh.vertices = vertices;
}
```

In the play mode the animation will start, modify the height and speed to farther customize the animation, the result should be like this :

Noise in particles system :
To generate outstanding images with minimal effort, the noise in video games expands even farther to the particles system. However, pelinNoise does not take place in the particles system, so another type of noise called Curl Noise is used. A Curl Noise uses several samples from a perlinNoise field.

To use your example, a Strength of 5 produces perlinNoise in the [-5,+5] range. Curl Noise then combines 2 samples for each axis, giving you a final range of [-10,+10].

This final value is the maximum potential units per second that any given particle may move.

The texture is used to demonstrate how the noise would effect the particles. Consider particles moving through noise (You are using Low Quality, in which we just generate one axis of noise and reuse it in all directions, for faster but less "interesting" noise). As the particles move through the noise, a grey area indicates no effect, a black area indicates a strong negative effect, and a white area indicates a significant positive effect.

A noise model in unity game engine have several functions like (strength, frequency , damping...etc).

To access the particle system noise you can do it either by inspector for simple functions or via script to farther customize your particles.

An example for the inspector is this panel :

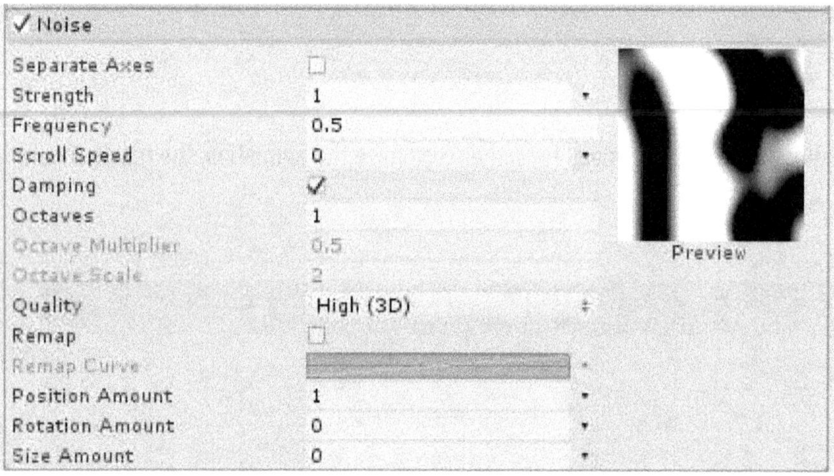

To access the particles from the script you need to require a component in a type of particle system and then in the start method you get the particle system component equals it to a variable and then modify as you need :

```
using UnityEngine;
using System.Collections;

[RequireComponent(typeof(ParticleSystem))]
public class ExampleClass : MonoBehaviour {
    void Start() {
        ParticleSystem ps = GetComponent<ParticleSystem>();
        var no = ps.noise;
        no.enabled = true;
        no.strength = 1.0f;
        no.quality = ParticleSystemNoiseQuality.High;
    }
}
```

Terrain Noise Editor :

The Noise Editor allows you to author and manage Noise Settings Assets, which you can use in the Noise Height Tool and Noise Brush Mask Filters. You can also use the Noise Editor to generate procedural textures. To open the Noise Editor, select Window-Terrain-Edit Noise.

We use the noise settings asset field to save and load curated Noise Settings assets. Note that there are two possible states :

- When no Noise Settings asset is allocated, Unity utilizes an internal instance of a Noise Settings asset, which can still be modified via the UI. Two buttons appear : Reset and Save As.
- When a Noise Settings asset is assigned, Unity duplicates the settings that are contained in that asset. When you adjust the noise settings in the UI, Unity only affects the copy of the Noise Settings file, not the actual Noise Settings asset on disk. As you update the settings, this prevents you from overwriting the original with undesirable changes. Three buttons appear : Revert, Apply and Save As.

We use the Transform Settings to move the noise domain space in the order of Translate, Rotate and Scale.

Translate : the noise's center space is moved from one location to another. Unity adds this translation value to the domain space input positions that the noise uses to build its output values. You may also do this by clicking and dragging the Noise Field Preview.

Rotate : rotates around the noise domain's origin, which Unity determines using the Translation value. Unity applies this rotation value to the domain space input positions that the noise uses to build its output values.

Scale :The domain space size of the input. Unity applies this scaling factor to the domain space input positions that the noise uses to build its output values. You can also do this action by moving the wheel button while the cursor is over the Noise Field Preview.

Flip Scale : Toggle the scale of the noise on the X, Y, and Z axes relative to the center of the Noise Field Preview using these buttons.

• X: Flips the patterns on the preview's right side to the left, and those on the preview's left side to the right.
• Y: Flips the patterns at the top of the preview to the bottom, and the bottom patterns to the top.
• Z: Because the preview is a 2D slice of the noise domain, there is no obvious effect. However, analogous to the Z axis of a camera, you can think of it as flipping an infinite pattern that enters and exits the preview.

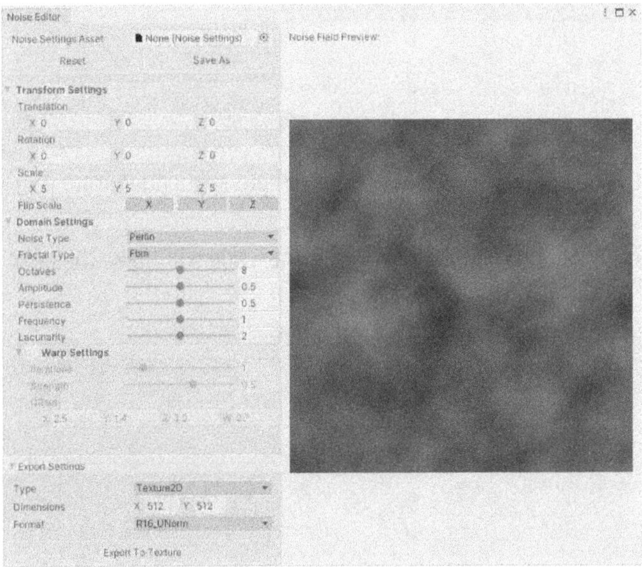

There is more Settings like (Domain Settings, Warp Settings, Export and Preview) in which you could adjust to make more complex noise.

Simple Noise Node :
we use the simple noise node which Generates a simple, or Value, noise based on input UV. The scale of the generated noise is controlled by input Scale, it consists of many ports like the following table :

Name	Direction	Type	Binding	Description
UV	Input	Vector 2	UV	Input UV value
Scale	Input	Vector 1	None	Noise scale
Out	Output	Vector 1	None	Output value

you could change it by code using some complicated functions like :

inline float : The float inline Operator allows you to save a float instance. This is one of the fundamental Types of the Visual Effect Graph. To change a value in this inline Operator, either explicitly set the value in the Operator body or connect it to a compatible output.

Yet using the nodes in unity is pretty much just math, like in this example it is used in the procedural part of the node library, so most of the code will usually be a mathf functions.

Gradient Noise :
it is a perlin noise based on input uv, the scale of the generated noise is controlled by the input scale, it also have many ports like the table below :

Name	Direction	Type	Binding	Description
UV	Input	Vector 2	UV	Input UV value
Scale	Input	Vector 1	None	Noise scale
Out	Output	Vector 1	None	Output value

now to use the knowledge we aquired in the use of noise inside the node library we will make a simple application from it.

We will start by making a 3d object like a cube and make a c# script called AnimatedNoiseColor this code will make the cube change its color with time according to a gradient.
To start we will make a float for scale and animation speed , also we need a gradient and a renderer :

```
public float scale = 0.1f;
public Gradient colorGradient;
public float animationSpeed = 1.0f;
private Renderer rend;
```

in the start method we get the renderer component :

```
Unity Message | 0 references
void Start()
{
    rend = GetComponent<Renderer>();
}
```

now we will make a noise random value float code :

```
4 references
float unity_noise_randomValue(Vector2 uv)
{
    return Mathf.Repeat(Mathf.Sin(Vector2.Dot(uv, new Vector2(12.9898f, 78.233f))) * 43758.5453f, 1.0f);
}
```

let's take apart this code in sections to understand it well , This code defines the unity_noise_randomValue function, which takes a 2D vector uv as input and returns a random value between 0 and 1 based on the input vector. This finction employs a "hashing" function, a simple pseudo-random number generation approach commonly used in computer graphics and procedural generation.

Here's a breakdown of how this function works step by step:

- Vector2.Dot(uv, new Vector2(12.9898f, 78.233f)): This section of code computes the dot product of the input vector uv and a constant vector (12.9898f, 78.233f). The dot product is a mathematical procedure that determines the cosine of the angle formed by two vectors. It is used in this situation to combine the values of the uv vector into a single scalar value.
- Mathf.Sin(...): The dot product result is then passed via the Mathf.Sin function, which computes the sine of the input value. This phase is used to induce non-linearity into the process.
- ... * 43758.5453f: The sine value is then multiplied by (43758.5453f). This multiplication helps to disperse the numbers more evenly and generate greater unpredictability.
- Mathf.Repeat(..., 1.0f): The multiplication result is finally passed through the Mathf.Repeat method. This method ensures that the result stays within the range [0, 1] by removing 1 from it continuously until it does.

Overall, this function takes a 2D input vector uv, runs it through a number of mathematical processes, and outputs a pseudo-random result between 0 (inclusive) and 1 (exclusive). This function is frequently used in computer graphics and procedural generation to generate pseudo-random patterns or noise that can be used to simulate natural processes or add variation to generated content.

And now we also need a float noise interpolate :

```
3 references
float unity_noise_interpolate(float a, float b, float t)
{
    return (1.0f - t) * a + t * b;
}
```

This code defines the function unity_noise_interpolate, which does linear interpolation (also abbreviated as "lerp") between two input values, a and b, based on a parameter t. Linear interpolation is a simple mathematical technique used to mix two values smoothly dependent on a third parameter.

Here's a breakdown of how this function works step by step:

- float a: This is the first input value, sometimes known as the "start" value.
- float b: This is the second input value, sometimes known as the "end" value.
- float t: The interpolation parameter, float t, controls how much of the value b is mixed with the value a. It's usually a value between 0 and 1, with 0 representing a and 1 representing b, and values in between creating a seamless transition between the two.

The function computes the result as follows:

- (1.0f - t) * a: This section computes the contribution based on the a value. It subtracts t from 1 and multiplies the result by a. When t is zero, (1.0f - t) equals one, therefore you obtain all of a. When t equals one, (1.0f - t) equals zero, therefore you get none of a. When t is between 0 and 1, a weighted combination of an is obtained.
- t * b: This section computes the contribution based on the b value. It divides t by b. When t is zero, you get none of the b. When t is 1, you obtain the entire value of b. When t is between 0 and 1, a weighted combination of b is obtained.
- (1.0f - t) * a + t * b: Finally, the sum of these two contributions yields the final interpolated value. The result smoothly goes from a to b as t changes between 0 and 1.

This linear interpolation function is useful in a variety of applications, including graphics, animation, and simulation, where smooth transitions between two values over time or space are desired. It's an essential building component in computer graphics and game development for creating animations, fades, and other smooth transitions.

Now we need to make a float value noise:

```
1 reference
float unity_valueNoise(Vector2 uv)
{
    Vector2 i = new Vector2(Mathf.Floor(uv.x), Mathf.Floor(uv.y));
    Vector2 f = new Vector2(uv.x - i.x, uv.y - i.y);
    f = f * f * (3.0f - 2.0f * f.x);

    uv = new Vector2(Mathf.Abs(uv.x - 0.5f), Mathf.Abs(uv.y - 0.5f));
    Vector2 c0 = i + new Vector2(0.0f, 0.0f);
    Vector2 c1 = i + new Vector2(1.0f, 0.0f);
    Vector2 c2 = i + new Vector2(0.0f, 1.0f);
    Vector2 c3 = i + new Vector2(1.0f, 1.0f);
    float r0 = unity_noise_randomValue(c0);
    float r1 = unity_noise_randomValue(c1);
    float r2 = unity_noise_randomValue(c2);
    float r3 = unity_noise_randomValue(c3);

    float bottomOfGrid = unity_noise_interpolate(r0, r1, f.x);
    float topOfGrid = unity_noise_interpolate(r2, r3, f.x);
    float t = unity_noise_interpolate(bottomOfGrid, topOfGrid, f.y);
    return t;
}
```

This code defines the function unity_valueNoise, which computes a 2D value noise using a grid-based sampling method. Value noise is a sort of noise used in computer graphics and procedural generation to generate random patterns that appear natural.

Here's a breakdown of how this function works step by step:

- Vector2 i = new Vector2(Mathf.Floor(uv.x), Mathf.Floor(uv.y)): This code computes the integer part of the input vector uv and puts it in the vector i. It essentially rounds down the uv coordinates to the nearest integer values.
- Vector2 f = new Vector2(uv.x - i.x, uv.y - i.y): This code computes the fractional part of the input vector uv by subtracting the integer part (i) from the original vector. This fractional portion represents the position within the grid cell.
- f = f * f * (3.0f - 2.0f * f.x): A smooth interpolation function is used to modify the fractional portion f here. This function smoothes the transitions between grid cells to provide a more natural-looking noise pattern.
- uv = new Vector2(Mathf.Abs(uv.x - 0.5f), Mathf.Abs(uv.y - 0.5f)): This code alters the input vector uv by taking the absolute difference between its components and 0.5. This step is frequently used to generate a more isotropic (directionally uniform) noise pattern.
- Vector2 c = i + new Vector2(0.0f, 0.0f): These lines compute the four grid cell corners that surround the changed uv position.
- float r = unity_noise_randomValue(c): Using the unity_noise_randomValue function, these lines compute random values (r0, r1, r2, and r3) for each of the four grid cell corners. These random values are utilized for interpolation.
- float bottomOfGrid & float topOfGrid: Linear interpolation is applied to the random values in the horizontal direction (f.x) to obtain values at the bottom and top of the grid cell.
- float t: Linear interpolation is used once more, this time in the vertical direction (f.y), to interpolate between the values obtained at the grid cell's bottom and top. The outcome is saved in t, and then we return the value of t.

Overall, this function takes an input vector uv, does grid-based sampling of random values, then interpolates between them to give a smooth value noise output. This can be used in graphics and procedural generation to create natural-looking textures or patterns.

Now in the update function we write the following:

```
Unity Message | 0 references
void Update()
{
    float noiseValue;
    Vector2 uv = new Vector2(transform.position.x, transform.position.z);

    noiseValue = unity_valueNoise(uv);

    float timeParameter = (Mathf.Sin(Time.time * animationSpeed) + 1.0f) / 2.0f;

    Color color = colorGradient.Evaluate(timeParameter);

    rend.material.color = color;
}
```

we simply declare the noise value and create a vector2 uv that is equal to the x and z positions, then we make the noise value equal to the unity_valueNoise function and pass in the uv, and finally we create a float time parameter that will calculate a value based on the current time and multiply it by the animation speed.

Note : the sin function is used to create a periodic oscillation of values between -1 and 1, which is then adjusted to be between 0 and 1 using the + 1.0f and then dividing it by 2.0f

and then we define the color and evaluate it according to the time parameter (so the color changes with time according to the gradient) , then we make the renderer material color equal to our color.

The result of this whole code should be a object that changes its color over time according to a gradient of colors :

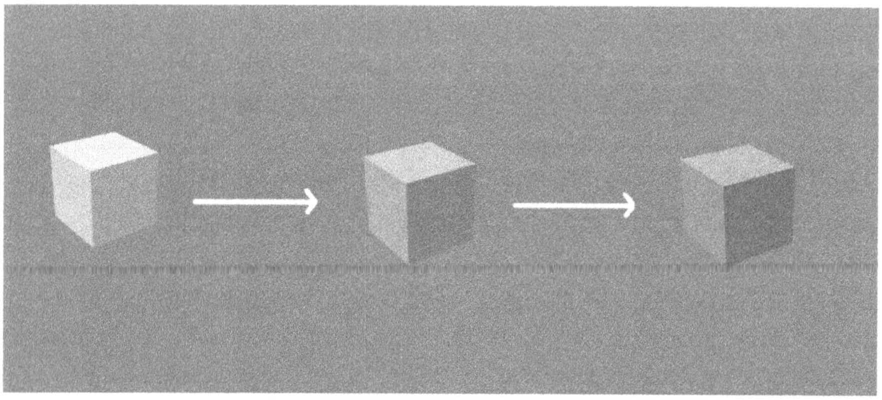

Chapter II
[DOTS]

DOTS (Data-Oriented Technology Stack): is considered advanced in the context of Unity game development. Unity DOTS is a set of technologies and techniques designed to optimize the performance and scalability of Unity games and simulations, particularly for projects that require high performance, massive numbers of entities, and complex simulations. It represents a departure from the traditional component-based architecture of Unity in favor of a data-oriented approach.

To show the difference in performance we will compare between a classic monobehaviours workflow and a ECS workflow (Entities, components, systems).

In the classic workflow we used a simple prefab generating script :

```
namespace DOTSCompare.Classic
{
    // This shows a "classic" movement System
    //
    //
    public class Movement : MonoBehaviour
    {
        // Update is called once per frame
        void Update()
        {

            Vector3 pos = transform.position;
            pos += transform.forward * GameManager.Instance.moveSpeed * Time.deltaTime;

            if (pos.z > GameManager.Instance.UpperBounds)
            {
                pos.z = GameManager.Instance.BottomBounds;
            }

            transform.position = pos;
        }
    }
}
```

we built around 15000 units in an average machine and hit around 27 to 30 frames per second.
If we used the ECS Pure we will git a 40000 units and hit around 26 to 30 frames per second in an average machine so around 2.5 times the classic with the same performance.
Either advantages that in ECS they are not a game objects they are Entities so we even have a more clear Hierarchy.
You can also make code to boost performance by using the device hardware so we take the advantages of having multiple cores cpu, in a several test using such codes increased the unites up to 160000 in a 29 to 31 frames per second if you activated the jobs and burst dot compiler.

You may not need 160000 objects in your screen in your game yet using DOTS is useful if applied because better performance means less power consumption and heat so your game will have a much better performance especially if it was for mobile or a laptop.

Creating Entities:
Make a new unity project, go to the project manager and install the Entities and Hybrid Renderer packages if wasn't installed but if you are higher than version 2019 you need to enable preview packages then add a git url of the package from unity Manual-Hybrid renderer manual [com.unity.rendering.hybrid].
Now make a new c# script and name it Spawner (or any other name that you want).
You have to add in the first of the script (using Unity.Entities) which we will need for the ECS.

Then we will make a void function that returns nothing called make Entity and call it in the start method:

```
using UnityEngine;
using Unity.Entities;

Unity Script | 0 references
public class Spawner : MonoBehaviour
{

    Unity Message | 0 references
    void Start()
    {
        MakeEntity();
    }

    1 reference
    private void MakeEntity()
    {

    }
}
```

to create an Entity we simply in the make entity function we all the entity manager using the world default game object injection method (current default world) and then call the entity manager create entity function:

```
1 reference
private void MakeEntity()
{
    EntityManager entityManager = World.DefaultGameObjectInjectionWorld.EntityManager;
    entityManager.CreateEntity();
}
```

now make an empty game object called spawner and add the script to it , in play mode we wont see difference because Entities does not show in the Hierarchy so you have to go to the Entity debugger window (or you can also use the DOTS hierarchy new window).

Now we need to add the (using unity transform, rendering and mathematics) :

```
using UnityEngine;
using Unity.Entities;
using Unity.Transforms;
using Unity.Rendering;
using Unity.Mathematics;
```

then we will use the entity arch type to define its type of Translation, rotation, mesh rendering and bounds and its location in the world:

```
EntityArchetype archetype = entityManager.CreateArchetype(
    typeof(Translation),
    typeof(Rotation),
    typeof(RenderMesh),
    typeof(RenderBounds),
    typeof(LocalToWorld)
    );
```

these are types that the Hybrid renderer requires to operate.
Now just pass the arch type in the create entity method:

```
entityManager.CreateEntity(archetype);
```

now you would see the changes in the entity debugger yet no object is seen in neither scene nor game view.
To solve this problem we need to get the mesh and material working in our create entity method:

```
[SerializeField] private Mesh unitMesh;
[SerializeField] private Material unitMaterial;
```

after making the unit mesh and the unit material a few changes should be made, first we will assign the entity manager create function to a my entity temporary then we will add component data for the translation using the float 3 function and add shared component data using the render mesh and the units of mesh and material that we defined before:

```
Entity myEntity = entityManager.CreateEntity(archetype);

entityManager.AddComponentData(myEntity, new Translation
{
    Value = new float3(2f, 0f, 4f)
});

entityManager.AddSharedComponentData(myEntity, new RenderMesh
{
    mesh = unitMesh,
    material = unitMaterial
```

then make a new material and make sure to check the enable GPU Instancing so the GPU will reduce the number of draw calls in our scene.
Assign the cube mesh (or any other mesh you want) with the material we made before in the spawner.

Conversion Workflow:

When converting an object to an entity in unity it disappears from the hierarchy and appears in the DOTS debugger / hierarchy.
You will also notice that it has the same arch type as our own generating entity function but with a one little small change which is the perInstanceCullingTag which is A tag component that allows for granular per-instance culling control.
When changing them to an entity you can move them in edit mode normally (because they only change to an entity in the game mode) so it is literally a "win win situation".
If you choose the convert and inject option you will get both the game object and the entity object.
Yet changing the status of an object from normal to an entity in runtime is quite different, first we make a new private Serialize filed of a game object prefab, then we make a private world, entity manager and entity prefab :

```
[SerializeField] private GameObject unitPrefab;

private Entity entityPerfab;
private World defaultWorld;
private EntityManager entityManager;
```

we will get the default world and the entity manager through the start method :

```
Unity Message | 0 references
void Start()
{
    defaultWorld = World.DefaultGameObjectInjectionWorld;
    entityManager = defaultWorld.EntityManager;
}
```

then in the start method we will define a variable called settings and make it equal to the conversion settings from the default world with the second argument being null, after that we make the entity prefab equals to the conversion utility and convert the unit prefab (the first argument) using the second argument which is the settings that we defined before:

```
GameObjectConversionSettings settings = GameObjectConversionSettings.
    FromWorld(defaultWorld, null);

entityPerfab = GameObjectConversionUtility.ConvertGameObjectHierarchy
    (unitPrefab, settings);
```

now we will make a new void function which is instantiate entity which is similar to what we did before, we will make an entity called my entity and equals it to the entity manager instantiate function and pass in the prefab, then take the data of the prefab position through the set component data function:

```
1 reference
private void InstantiateEntity(float3 position)
{
    Entity myEntity = entityManager.Instantiate(entityPerfab);
    entityManager.SetComponentData(myEntity, new Translation
    {
        Value = position
    });
}
```

and then we call the instantiate entity function inside the start method and passing the location:

```
InstantiateEntity(new float3(4f, 0f, 4f));
```

now for further exploring lets make a grid using entities, first we will make a void called instantiate entity grid, with two int arguments one for the dimensions of x, one for y and one float for spacing, then we will make two for loops with the lengths being the dimensions, then we instantiate the entity and call the function in the start method instead of the instantiate entity:

```
1 reference
private void InstantiateEntityGrid(int dimX , int dimY, float spacing = 1f)
{
    for (int i = 0; i < dimX; i++)
    {
        for (int j = 0; j < dimY; j++)
        {
            InstantiateEntity(new float3(i * spacing, j * spacing, 0f));
        }
    }
}
```

```
InstantiateEntityGrid(10, 10, 1f);
```

the result in the play mode should be a grid of 100 cube entities.
You can even further customize by adding the dimX , dimY and spacing in a serialized field so you can modify them from the inspector.

DOTS Components and Systems:

Entities are processed by systems in DOTS. You create systems that operate on entities and query for specific entities based on their components. For example, you might have a movement system that queries for all entities with a "Position Component" and updates their positions based on their velocities.
to explain it in application we will make our entities move so we will make a system for motion.
Make two new folders one for systems and one for data and inside the data folder make a move speed data c# script.
You should add using unity entities and the script should inherit from IComponentData instead of monobehaviour and it should be a struct instead of a class.
And now simply add a public float called Value:

```
using Unity.Entities;

0 references
public struct MoveSpeedData : IComponentData
{
    public float Value;
```

yet if you try adding the script to an object it will show an error so make sure to use Generate Authoring Component:

```
[GenerateAuthoringComponent]
```

now add the script to the prefab so each time it gets instantiated a move speed data is added to the entity.
Now make a new c# script in the system folder and call it wave system add unity entities, transform and mathematics and make it Component system instead of monobehaviour and then generate an abstract class:

```
using Unity.Entities;
using Unity.Transforms;
using Unity.Mathematics;

0 references
public class WaveSystem : ComponentSystem
{
    0 references
    protected override void OnUpdate()
    {

    }
}
```

then use the entities for each function to get the transform of every entity and then we will set a float that is called zPosition and make it equal to math sin function and we will use the time ECS elapsed time which is a double now in our example we want the cubes to move only in the z axis but stay in other axis position so we will assign the trans Value to a new float 3 :

```
float zPosition = math.sin((float)Time.ElapsedTime);
trans.Value = new float3(trans.Value.x, trans.Value.y, zPosition);
```

now in the play mode the cubes grid should change position in the z axis only.
Also you can reference the move speed data and multiply its value to the elapsed time:

```
Entities.ForEach((ref Translation trans, ref MoveSpeedData moveSpeed) =>
{
    float zPosition = math.sin((float)Time.ElapsedTime * moveSpeed.Value);
    trans.Value = new float3(trans.Value.x, trans.Value.y, zPosition);
});
```

now to make things a bit more interesting we will modify the sine wave using the amplitude , the angular frequency and the phase shift:

Sine wave

$$y(t) = A\sin(\omega t + \varphi)$$

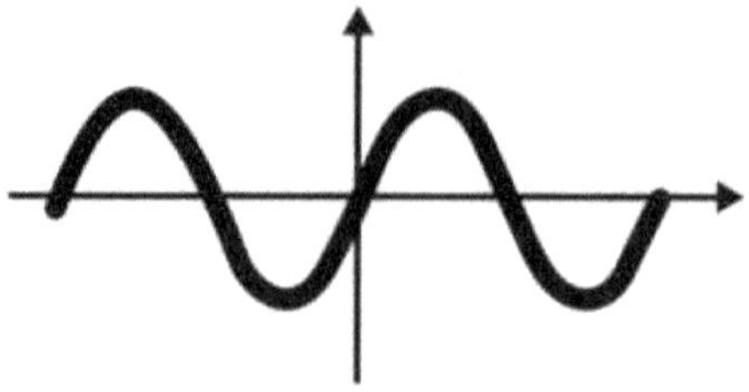

A = amplitude

ω = angular frequency

φ = phase shift

now in order to use that we will make a new data script called wave data.
The structure of the code is similar to the move speed data :

```
using Unity.Entities;

[GenerateAuthoringComponent]
5 references
public struct WaveData : IComponentData
{
    public float amplitude;
    public float xOffset;
    public float yOffset;
}
```

and then add the script to the prefab, now in the wave system reference the wave data and then multiply the wave data amplitude to the math sin function and then add the Xoffset and Yoffset to the move speed value:

```
Entities.ForEach((ref Translation trans, ref MoveSpeedData moveSpeed, ref WaveData waveData) =>
{
    float zPosition = waveData.amplitude * math.sin((float)Time.ElapsedTime * moveSpeed.Value
        + trans.Value.x * waveData.xOffset + trans.Value.y * waveData.yOffset);
    trans.Value = new float3(trans.Value.x, trans.Value.y, zPosition);
});
```

and in the play mode a very smooth flag-like animation is added to the entities.
Here is some sample settings for the animation [amplitude = 5 , Xoffset = 0.25, Yoffset = 0.25].

Job Systems:

Unity's job system allows you to write multithreaded code that can operate on all available CPU cores. This improves performance because your application uses the capability of all the CPU cores it is executing on more efficiently, rather than running all code on one CPU core.

You can use the job system on its own, but for better performance, you should also utilize the Burst compiler, which is specifically built to build jobs for Unity's job system. The Burst compiler has enhanced code generation, resulting in faster performance and lower energy use for mobile devices.
You may also combine the task system with Unity's Entity Component System to develop high-performance data-oriented programs.

Multithreading:

Unity processes its own native code over several worker threads, the number of which depends on the number of CPU cores available on the device your program runs on. Typically, Unity executes your code on the main thread, which runs by default at the start of the application. When you use the job system, Unity executes your code over several worker threads, which is known as multithreading.
multithreading makes use of a CPU's capacity to process several threads at once across multiple cores. Tasks or instructions are executed concurrently rather than sequentially. The worker threads run concurrently and synchronize their results with the main thread once completed.
The job system ensures that there are just enough threads to meet the capacity of the CPU cores, so you can plan as many jobs as you need without knowing how many CPU cores are available. This differs from other task systems that rely on techniques like thread pooling, where it is easy to create more threads than CPU cores inefficiently.

Work stealing:

Work stealing is used by the job system as part of its scheduling technique to balance out the quantity of tasks shared between worker threads. Worker threads may process jobs quicker than others, so once a worker thread has completed all of its duties, it checks the queues of other worker threads and then processes tasks allocated to another worker thread.

Safety system:

To make it easier to develop multithreaded code, the task system includes a safety layer that detects all potential race circumstances and protects you from the errors they can cause. A race condition occurs when the outcome of one operation is dependent on the timing of another activity that is not within its control.

For example, if the job system transmits a reference to data from your code in the main thread to a job, it cannot verify whether the main thread is reading the data at the same time the job is writing to it. This scenario produces a race condition.

To address this issue, the job system delivers each job a copy of the data it needs to work on rather than a reference to the data in the main thread and this copy isolates the data which eliminates the race condition.
Because of the way the job system transfers data, a job can only access blittable data types. When passed between managed and native code, these types do not require conversion.

Memcpy is used by the task system to copy blittable types and move data between the managed and native components of Unity. for scheduling jobs, it utilizes memcpy to copy data into native memory and offers the managed side access to that copy for running jobs. See Job Scheduling for further information.
Job system in application:
make a new c# script called "Example" and use the unity jobs and the unity collections, also you can remove the update method because we wont use it, and make a new method called "DoExample" and then call it in the start mehod:

```
using System.Collections;
using Unity.Jobs;
using UnityEngine;


Unity Message | 0 references
void Start()
{
    DoExample();
}

1 reference
private void DoExample()
{

}
```

this is what we usually deal with using the normal monobehaviour scripts which is single threaded, now to set it up to the worker threads we need to set up a job so first we make a private struct which implements our job:

```
0 references
private struct SimpleJob : IJob
{
    0 references
    public void Execute()
    {
        //the logic of the job
    }
}
```

a job could contain things like floats and native arrays of float so lets make them and declare the first float of the array to the value of the other float:

```
public float a;

public NativeArray<float> result;

0 references
public void Execute()
{
    //the logic of the job
    result[0] = a;
}
```

now to use a job we need a bit extra steps first is to instantiate the job then initialize the instance and after that schedule the job , this is an example code of how it should look like:

```
1 reference
private void DoExample()
{
    NativeArray<float> resultArray = new NativeArray<float>(1, Allocator.TempJob);

    //Instatiate and Initialize
    SimpleJob job = new SimpleJob
    {
        a = 5f,
        result = new NativeArray<float>(1, Allocator.TempJob)

    };

    //schedule
    JobHandle handle = job.Schedule();

    //other tasks to run in the main thread in parallel
    handle.Complete();

    float resultingValue = resultArray[0];
    Debug.Log("result" + resultingValue);

    resultArray.Dispose();
}
```

now add the script to a game object and on play mode the result should appear on the console.

You can play around with this code and even apply it in any other code to boost performance by using the multiple threads on the CPU.

The Entity Component System (ECS) in Unity provides several key advantages that make it an appealing alternative for game creators, particularly when dealing with performance-critical applications. Here are some of the main advantages of using ECS in Unity:

- High Performance: ECS is optimized for performance and scalability. It makes use of data-oriented design concepts and supports efficient multi-threading.
  For improved multi-core CPU performance, the Unity Job System and Burst Compiler are used.
  Reduces cache misses while increasing CPU cache use, resulting in quicker execution times.
- Scalability: Suitable for dealing with a high number of entities (things) in a scenario without causing substantial performance reduction Allows for the efficient management of hundreds, if not millions, of entities at the same time.
- Parallel Processing: Automatically schedules jobs across many CPU cores to allow for concurrent execution of game logic. Perfect for CPU-intensive operations like as physics simulations, AI calculations, and graphics.
- Decoupling of Logic and Data: Separates game logic (Systems) from data (Components), allowing for a more streamlined and flexible code structure. Improves code reusability, maintainability, and developer collaboration.
- Flexibility: Allows for the creation of both 2D and 3D games, as well as a wide range of genres and project sizes. Can be used in conjunction with classic MonoBehaviour-based components to provide a hybrid approach.
- Optimized Memory Usage: Components are stored in a compact memory arrangement, which reduces memory overhead. Through the Entity and ComponentData structures, effective memory allocation and management is possible.
- Custom Data Layouts: Developers have complete control over data storage, allowing for customized data layouts to meet specific performance requirements. Allows programmers to align data structures with cache lines for faster memory access...etc

And there is much more and more uses and advantages.

CHAPTER III
[Editor Scripting]

The process of creating custom tools, extensions, and functionality expressly for use within the Unity Editor is referred known as editor scripting. These scripts let you to automate processes, improve workflow, and create custom inspectors, windows, and utilities for your Unity projects. Editor scripting can be used for a variety of activities like level design, data management, debugging, and more.
Editor scripting can help you be more productive in Unity by making it easier to build, manage, and debug your projects. Unity's editor scripting API is robust and adaptable, allowing you to create a variety of custom tools and extensions suited to your individual needs.

Creating a window:

We will start by making a c# script called Designer window, and for management make a folder called editor and move the script inside the folder.
Now inside the script we use the unity editor and delete the monobehaviour and use the editorwindow method:

```
using System.Collections;
using UnityEngine;
using UnityEditor;

Unity Script | 0 references
public class DesignerWindow : EditorWindow
{

}
```

now lets make a static function called open window, and it should have the menu item attribute above it which will pass a string value which defines where this function is accessible via the tool bar. So for example we want it to be accessible from window then designer:

```
[MenuItem("Window/Designer")]
0 references
static void openWindow()
{

}
```

now lets make a script for the get window call , we will make a new window and set it equals to our class type and then call get window which will be a type of designer window. And then we will set the window min size so it never be too small to see:

```
0 references
static void openWindow()
{
    DesignerWindow window = (DesignerWindow)GetWindow(typeof(DesignerWindow));
    window.minSize = new Vector2(600, 300);
}
```

you can also make a window max size if you want, now we just need to use the function window show so it show in the editor:

```
window.Show();
```

and now inside unity Window you should see a new window called Designer and when you click a window will show:

Scriptable Objects:

first let's make a simple setup so it looks more organized and similar to a real game project, you need to make two folders one for the prefabs which will have a folder of characters containing a mage, rogue and a warrior , the other file is called resources which will have two folders one for the characters data , it contains a data file that contains mage, rogue and warrior files, the other folder is scripts which contain 4 c# scripts , one for the character data , one for mage data, rogue data and the warrior data:

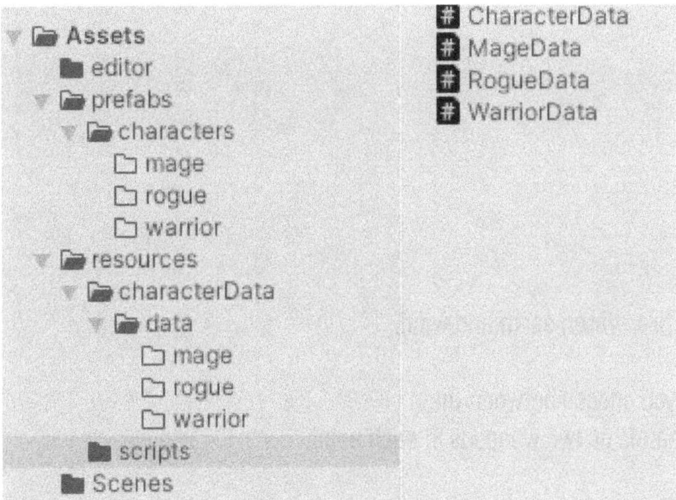

also we need a script outside the resources that is also called scripts which contains a c# for Mage, Rogue , Warrior and Types:

now inside the types script first we will use it as a name space which contains multiple enums for the mage , rogue and warrior class, weapons, damage type and also strategy just like any other simple game project:

```
namespace Types
{
    0 references
    public enum MageDamageTy
        FIRE,
        EARTH
    }

    0 references
    public enum MageWeaponTy
    {
        STAFF,
        WAND
    }

    0 references
    public enum WarriorClas:
    {
        DEFENDER,
        BERSERKER
    }

    0 references
    public enum WarriorWeapc
    {
        ONE_HANDED_SWORD,
        TWO_HANDED_SWORD,
        DUAL_WIELDED_SWORD
    }

    0 references
    public enum RogueWeapon1
    {
        DAGERS,
        BOW
    }

    0 references
    public enum RogueStrate(
    {
        STEALTH,
        SPEED
    }
}
```

Now the damage type of mage could contain its abilities like fire, water, earth and wind.
The mage weapon contains a staff or a wand usually.
A warrior could be a defender or a Berserker in this code so you choose between them.
The weapon of the warrior could be held in one hand or two hands or two weapons in each hand.
The rogue could either use dagers or bow in this code.
And you can choose his strategy if he will rush into enemies or stealth.
Now inside the mage script we need to reference the mage data script in order they work together like this:

```
Unity Script | 0 references
public class Mage : MonoBehaviour
{
    public MageData mageData;
}
```

now repeat this process for the rogue and the warrior, and then we will start working on our data classes and here where we want to use scriptable objects.

So inside the character data instead of using monobehaviour we will use the scriptableObject method:

```
public class CharacterData : ScriptableObject
{

}
```

then we have to reference the prefab, and make a float for the max health, max stamina, critical chance, power and a string variable for the name:

```
public GameObject prefab;
public float maxHealth;
public float maxStamina;
public float criticalChance;
public float power;
public string name;
```

now in other data classes we will reference the character data instead of monobehaviour and then on top we will write using types name space which we made before, the mage script will access the mage weapon and damage:

```
using System.Collections;
using System.Collections.Generic;
using UnityEngine;
using Types;

Unity Script | 1 reference
public class MageData : CharacterData
{
    public MageDamageType DamageType;
    public MageWeaponType WeaponType;
}
```

now to make our scriptable object visible in the create function in the unity editor when to make an attribute in the top of the class called create asset menu attribute and then assign the file name you want:

```
[CreateAssetMenu(fileName = "New Mage Data")]
```

also you can assign a menu name in the code like character data/mage and then apply the same script concept for the rogue and warrior.

Now when you create the scriptable object it will look like this :

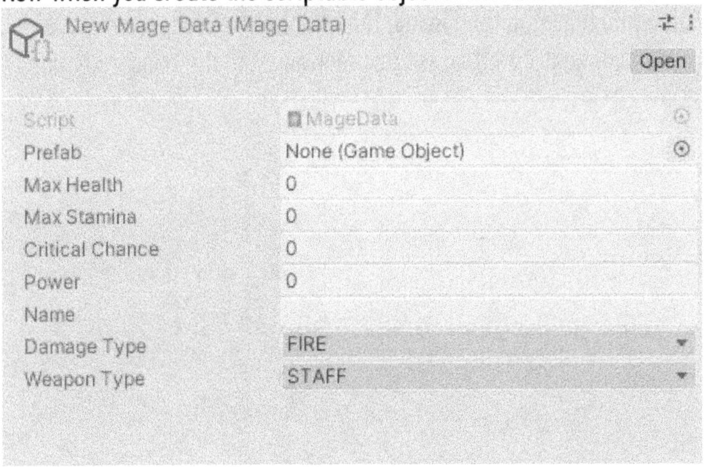

Layouts and color:

So we will start from where we left before in the designer window, we will make a texture 2d for the header, mage, rogue and warrior, a color variable for the header selection bar and a rectangle (for the header, mage, rogue and the warrior):

```
Texture2D headerSectionTexture;
Texture2D mageSectionTexture;
Texture2D rogueSectionTexture;
Texture2D warriorSectionTexture;

Color headerSectionColor = new Color(13f / 255f, 32f / 255f, 44f / 255f, 1f);

Rect headerSection;
Rect mageSection;
Rect rogueSection;
Rect warriorSection;
```

now we will make several functions on is on enable which is similar to start or awake functions, an initialize textures function, on GUI function, Draw layouts function and draw header, mage settings, rogue settings and warrior settings:

```
0 references
void DrawLayouts()
{

}

0 references
void DrawHeader()
{

}

0 references
void DrawMageSettings()
{

}
```

we will call the initialize textures function inside the on enable function, and then inside the initialize textures we make a new texture for the header using the texture method in unity and make it 1 x 1 then set its color equal to the header section color and then just apply the texture:

```
1 reference
void InitTextures()
{
    headerSectionTexture = new Texture2D(1, 1);
    headerSectionTexture.SetPixel(0, 0, headerSectionColor);
    headerSectionTexture.Apply();
}
```

and inside the on GUI function we will call the other five functions:

```
0 references
void OnGUI()
{
    DrawLayouts();
    DrawHeader();
    DrawMageSettings();
    DrawRogueSettings();
    DrawWarriorSettings();
}
```

now we will define the header sections position by using its x and y position in the screen and equal its width to the width of the screen and its height to 50 or any value you would like to use, after that we will use the GUI draw texture function in which we will pass the header section and texture:

```
1 reference
void DrawLayouts()
{
    headerSection.x = 0;
    headerSection.y = 0;
    headerSection.width = Screen.width;
    headerSection.height = 50;

    GUI.DrawTexture(headerSection, headerSectionTexture);
}
```

now in the same we we just initialize the other draw for mage, rogue and the warrior and then call them on the GUI function:

```
Unity Message | 0 references
void OnGUI()
{
    DrawLayouts();
    DrawHeader();
    DrawMageSettings();
    DrawRogueSettings();
    DrawWarriorSettings();
}
```

```
mageSectionTexture = new Texture2D(512, 512);
rogueSectionTexture = new Texture2D(512, 512);
warriorSectionTexture = new Texture2D(512, 512);
```

then we will define there position and value too inside the draw layout function:

```
//mage
mageSection.x = 0;
mageSection.y = 50;
headerSection.width = Screen.width / 3f;
headerSection.height = Screen.width - 50;

//rogue
rogueSection.x = (Screen.width / 3f) * 2;
rogueSection.y = 50;
rogueSection.width = Screen.width / 3f;
rogueSection.height = Screen.width - 50;

//warrior
warriorSection.x = Screen.width / 3f;
warriorSection.y = 50;
warriorSection.width = Screen.width / 3f;
warriorSection.height = Screen.width - 50;

GUI.DrawTexture(headerSection, headerSectionTexture);
GUI.DrawTexture(mageSection, mageSectionTexture);
GUI.DrawTexture(rogueSection, rogueSectionTexture);
GUI.DrawTexture(warriorSection, warriorSectionTexture);
```

you can also make the header using the GUI layout begin and end area function:

```
1 reference
void DrawHeader()
{
    GUILayout.BeginArea(headerSection);

    GUILayout.EndArea();
}
```

Labels:

They are text or descriptions that can be displayed within custom GUI controls in the Unity Inspector or custom Editor Windows in Unity Editor scripting. Labels are used to provide context or information to the user, making the Unity Editor and your own tools easier to understand and work with.

Here are some common uses of labels in Unity Editor scripting:

- Inspector Labels: Labels can be used to display information about the fields or attributes you're modifying while developing custom inspectors for your scripts. These labels assist users in understanding the function of each field.
- Custom Editor Windows: Labels are used in custom Editor Windows to give headings, descriptions, or explanations for various aspects of your window's interface.
- Custom GUI Controls: Labels can be added to various custom GUI controls such as buttons, sliders, and text fields to give the user with context or descriptions.

Labels serve a crucial part in delivering a user-friendly interface in custom inspectors and Editor Windows, allowing developers and artists to work more easily with Unity and your custom tools. They can assist in clarifying the function of various editor features, enhancing the overall usability of your projects.

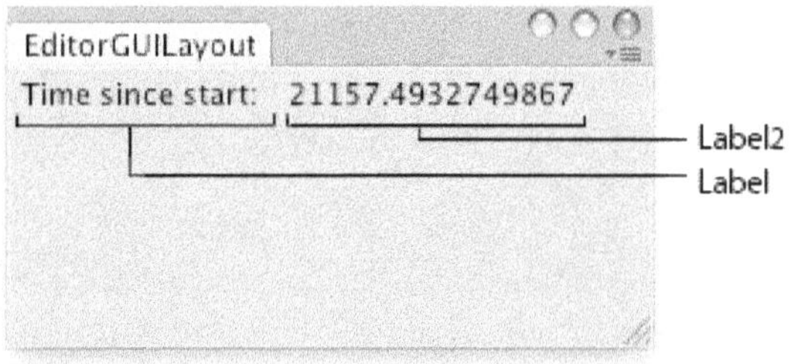

Enumerations:

Enums (short for enumerations) are a powerful approach to provide a variety of predefined alternatives for various attributes, fields, and settings within the Unity Inspector or custom Editor Windows in Unity Editor scripting. Enums allow developers and users to choose from a variety of discrete and meaningful options without having to remember or write individual values. They can represent a set of connected alternatives or states.

Here's how you can use enums in Unity Editor scripting:

- Defining Enums: An enum type is defined by creating a new C# enumeration. Each enumeration member indicates a distinct choice or state.
- Enums in Components: Enums can be used as fields in MonoBehaviour scripts to represent several states or modes for your game or component.
- Inspector Use: When you use enums in a MonoBehaviour script, Unity creates a dropdown menu in the Inspector that allows you to select one of the defined enum values. This allows designers and developers to easily select from the various options.
- Custom Editor Scripts: You can construct custom GUI controls to display and modify enums in custom editor scripts. You can, for example, use EditorGUILayout.To construct a dropdown for picking an enum value, use EnumPopup.
- Script Logic: You can utilize the selected enum value to affect the behavior or state of your components in your scripts, providing a straightforward approach to describe different modes or options.

In summary, enums are very effective when representing discrete, distinct alternatives, such as game states, character classes, or several types of things. You may improve the user experience in the Unity Inspector, make your code more clear, and verify that legitimate and relevant values are utilized by utilizing enums.

Enums in Unity Editor scripting aid in the organization and presentation of options and states in a clear and user-friendly manner, both in the Inspector and custom Editor Windows, and they simplify the logic and design of your game components.

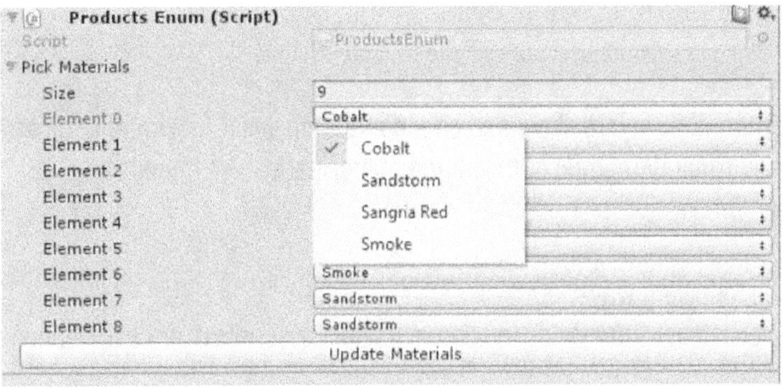

Buttons:

Buttons are GUI controls in Unity Editor scripting that allow you to activate custom actions or functions in response to user interaction. To develop interactive tools and extensions, these buttons can be attached to custom Editor Windows, Inspector custom editors, or other GUI elements in the Unity Editor. Buttons are a convenient approach to create user-friendly interfaces for activating activities without having to manually write code or utilize keyboard shortcuts.

In Unity Editor scripting, you may use buttons as follows:

- Custom Inspector Buttons: You can use EditorGUILayout to generate buttons in custom Inspector scripts.Button for performing actions on the viewed object.

- Custom Editor Windows: You can use the GUI to build buttons in custom Editor Windows.The button or the GUILayout.Button for creating tools with user-defined actions. These buttons can be used to carry out a variety of functions within your customized windows.
- Script Logic: You can utilize buttons in your scripts to initiate functions, methods, or actions. In a custom editor script, for example, you can use the button to initiate a specific procedure or computation.
- Conditional Logic: Buttons can be used in conjunction with conditional logic to give context-specific actions. You can activate or disable buttons based on the current state of your object or application.
- Toolbar Buttons: Toolbar buttons in Unity Editor windows allow you to transition between multiple perspectives or tools.

Buttons are vital in Unity Editor programming for generating user-friendly tools and interfaces that allow users to interact with and trigger activities without having to learn complex keyboard keys or write commands. They are an essential component of the visual development process, allowing users to interact with your custom tools and extensions in a natural manner.

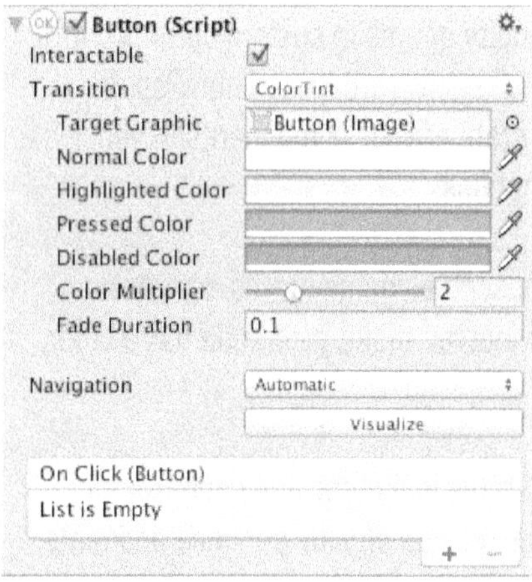

Float Fields:

In Unity Editor programming, float fields are GUI controls that allow you to show and change floating-point (decimal) numbers in the editor. These fields are frequently used to give a user-friendly method of modifying numerical values linked with attributes or components in the Inspector or custom Editor Windows.

Float fields can be used in Unity Editor programming in the following ways:

- Custom Inspector:EditorGUILayout can be used to construct float fields in custom Inspector scripts.Users can change float values associated with an item using FloatField.
- Custom Editor Windows: You can use EditorGUI to generate float fields in custom Editor Windows.FloatField or EditorGUILayout are two options.FloatField. These fields can be used for a variety of tasks, including setting properties and developing custom tools that require numerical input.
- Script Logic: Float fields can be used to express and alter numerical values within your custom components, which is very handy when developing tools or systems that require numerical input.
- Range Adjustments: Float fields can be used to set the attributes and parameters of various components, allowing users to change settings such as position, scale, speed, or other numerical properties.
- Data Input: Float fields are handy for inputting and manipulating data in bespoke tools, as well as for numerical control over different parts of your project.

Float fields are versatile and are often utilized in Unity Editor scripting for any case when you need to input or adjust floating-point data. They provide a visual and user-friendly way to edit numeric attributes, settings, and parameters within the Unity Editor, which is useful for both designing games and creating custom tools and extensions.

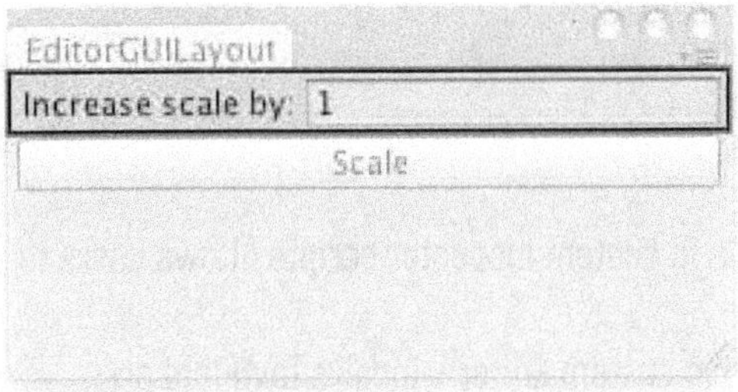

Slider fields:

Slider fields are GUI controls in Unity Editor programming that allow you to provide a visual way to alter numerical values within a specified range using a slider. They are a simple way to establish and view numerical properties or parameters, such as variables that indicate settings such as volume, brightness, or any other value that can be altered within a particular range.

Here's how you can use Slider fields in Unity Editor scripting:

- Custom Inspector: Slider fields can be created in custom Inspector scripts using EditorGUILayout.A slider that allows users to change float or integer numbers within a given range.
- Custom Editor Windows: Slider fields in custom Editor Windows can be created with EditorGUI.Slider or EditorGUILayout.Slider. Users can set and visualize numeric properties within specified ranges using these fields.
- Custom Tool Tips: You may add tooltips to Slider fields to provide users with more information or explanations about the slider's purpose and the allowable range of values.
- Script Logic: Slider fields can be used to express and alter numeric properties or parameters within your custom components or tools, particularly where a visual representation is advantageous for user engagement.
- Range Adjustments: Slider fields are useful for configuring and modifying attributes with a defined range, such as audio volume, brightness, opacity, or any other numerical value within a given range.
- Data Fine-Tuning: Slider fields are useful for precise fine-tuning of values, which is particularly important for creating polished game assets and tools.

Slider fields provide a simple and user-friendly mechanism for users to change numerical values within predefined ranges. They're often used in Unity Editor scripting to make it easier for users to engage with your custom tools and extensions by making it easy to define numeric parameters and settings.

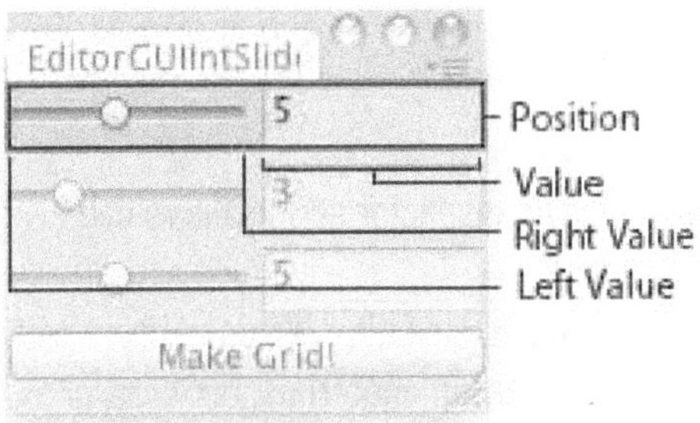

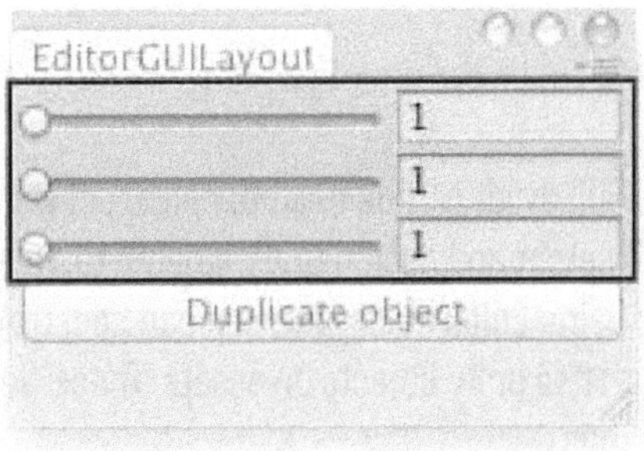

Text fields:

Text fields are GUI controls in Unity Editor scripting that allow you to display and edit text or string values in the Unity Editor. Text fields are frequently used to give easy-to-use input and display options for properties, component settings, or custom tools.

Here's how you can use Text fields in Unity Editor scripting:

- Custom Inspector: EditorGUILayout can be used to construct text fields in custom Inspector scripts.Allows users to enter or change string values linked with an object via a TextField.
- Custom Editor Windows: Using EditorGUI, you can construct text fields in custom Editor Windows.TextField or EditorGUILayout are two options.TextField. These fields can be used for a variety of reasons, including setting settings and developing custom tools that require text input.
- Script Logic: Text fields can be used to represent and alter string values within your custom components. This is beneficial for developing tools or systems that require textual input.
- Data Input: Text fields can be used to enter text data, such as identifying game objects, providing file paths, or providing custom descriptions.
- Error Messages and Feedback: Text fields can be used to display error messages, user feedback, or other textual information to users.

Within the Unity Editor, text fields provide an easy way to enter and change string values. They provide a user-friendly interface for textual input and are often used in Unity Editor scripting to construct tools, components, and custom windows that let users to work with text-based data or information.

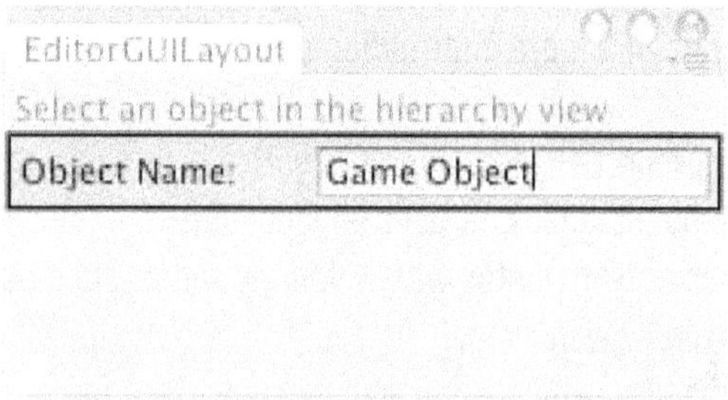

Object fields:

Object fields in Unity Editor scripting are GUI controls that allow you to choose and assign Unity objects such as GameObjects, Prefabs, Materials, Textures, Scripts, and more within the Unity Editor. Object fields are a convenient way to reference and allocate assets or game objects within custom inspectors, Editor Windows, or other UI components.

Here's how you can use Object fields in Unity Editor scripting:

- Custom Inspector: EditorGUILayout can be used to construct Object fields in custom Inspector scripts.Users can utilize the ObjectField to select and assign Unity objects to an object or component.
- Custom Editor Windows: Using EditorGUILayout, you can construct Object fields in custom Editor Windows.Users can use the ObjectField to refer to Unity objects or assets. These fields can be used to assign materials, textures, or prefabs, among other things.

- Script Logic: Within your custom components or tools, you can use Object fields to reference and interact with Unity objects and assets. This is important when developing tools or systems that need to refer to game objects, materials, or other assets.
- Prefab Assignment: Object fields are widely used to assign and reference prefabs and other resources, making it simple to spawn or instantiate them within scripts.
- Scene Hierarchy Integration: When an Object field refers to a GameObject or Transform, it integrates with the scene hierarchy, allowing users to select objects directly from the scene view.

Object fields make it simple for users to connect different parts in a project by allowing them to reference and assign Unity objects and assets. They are required for the development of custom inspectors, editor windows, and tools that need the selection or assignment of Unity objects and assets.

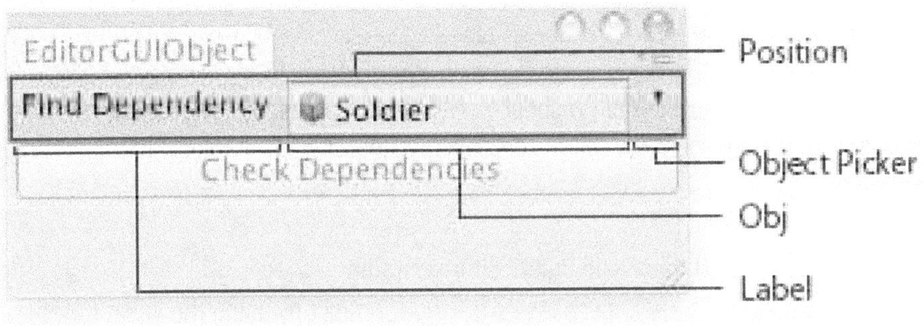

Help Boxes:

Help boxes are GUI controls in Unity Editor scripting that allow you to display useful messages, hints, or documentation to provide help and explanations to users working with your custom tools, components, or extensions. Help boxes are commonly used in the Unity Editor to provide context, instructions, or clarifications on how to utilize or customize a specific feature or function.

Here's how you can use Help Boxes in Unity Editor scripting:

- Custom Inspector: EditorGUILayout can be used to build Help boxes in custom Inspector scripts.A HelpBox is used to display information about a component's features or capabilities.
- Custom Editor Windows: GUI.Box or EditorGUILayout can be used to build Help boxes in custom Editor Windows.utilize the HelpBox to show users explanations, hints, or tips on how to utilize your tools or extensions.
- MessageType: The MessageType argument lets you choose the style or kind of the Help window. MessageType is one of the choices available in Unity.MessageType for general information.MessageType and Warning for warnings.Error message for error messages. You can select the suitable type based on the information you wish to express.

Help boxes can be used to provide user-friendly explanations, recommendations, and guidance to users who are working with your custom tools, components, or extensions. They are critical for improving your tools' usability and accessibility, as well as ensuring that users understand how to engage with your special features.

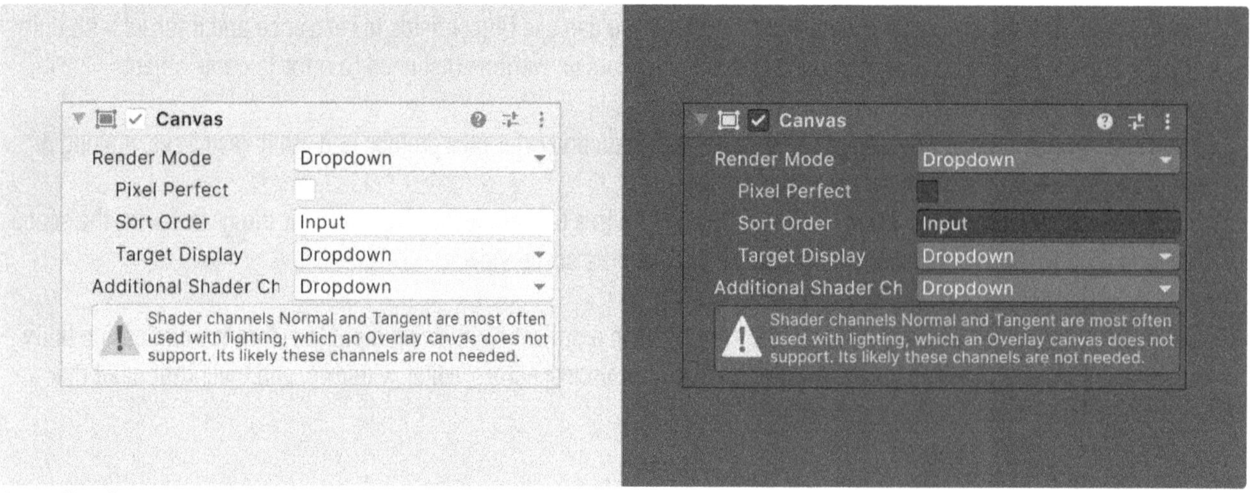

Asset Database:

The "Asset Database" in Unity Editor programming refers to a set of procedures and tools supplied by Unity for maintaining and querying assets within your Unity project. It enables you to directly execute asset import, export, import settings, and asset queries from your custom Editor scripts.

Here are some of the core features and uses of the Asset Database in Unity Editor scripting:

- Asset Import and Reimport: You can programmatically import assets into your project by using the Asset Database. This is very beneficial for automating asset import operations. You may also use asset reimport to update asset settings.
- Asset Query and Search: The Asset Database includes utilities for searching and querying assets in your project. This allows you to look for assets based on their name, kind, label, and other parameters. This is extremely important for creating custom asset management or organizing solutions.
- Asset Serialization and Database Updates: The Asset Database tracks changes to your project's assets. Functions can be used to regulate and optimize serialization, which is useful for batch processing assets or enhancing project performance.
- Asset Labels and Metadata: Labels and metadata can be assigned to assets, making it easier to organize, categorize, and filter objects inside the project. This might be useful when developing custom asset management solutions.
- Asset Export and Building: The Asset Database can be used to create assets for various platforms or to provide bespoke export functions.

The Asset Database is a powerful capability for working with assets within Unity Editor scripting, making it easy to construct custom asset management tools, automate asset-related processes, and optimize your Unity project's workflow.

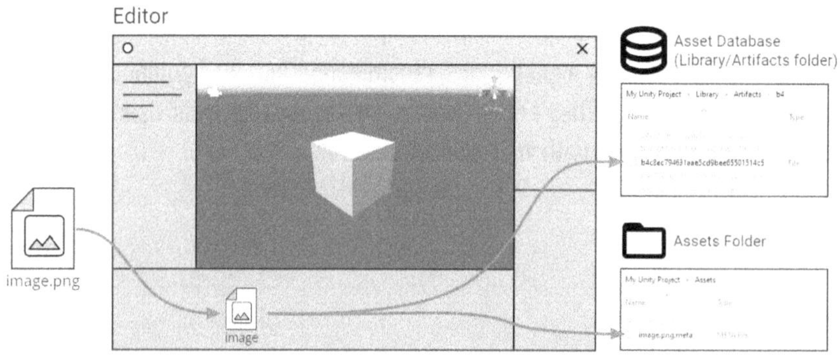

CHAPTER IV
[Scripting Patterns]

Scripting patterns are design patterns in software development that are widely utilized to tackle reoccurring difficulties or challenges when developing code. They offer structured and tested solutions to common problems, making code more maintainable, reusable, and understandable. Scripting patterns can help you write cleaner, more efficient, and more organized code in the context of Unity game development or any other programming work. Here are some examples of popular scripting patterns used in Unity and other programming environments.

The Singleton pattern assures that a class only has one instance and gives a global point of access to that instance. This can be used in Unity for building a central manager for game settings, resource loading, and other global functions.

The Factory design decouples the process of creating objects from the rest of the code. It's useful for producing complex items, especially when the process varies or involves numerous steps.

The Observer pattern is used in the implementation of event handling systems. It enables one object (the subject) to inform other objects (observers) of changes without knowing who or what those observers are. This pattern is common in Unity's event system.

The Command pattern encapsulates a request as an object, allowing for request customization, request queuing, and request logging. This method can be used to provide undo/redo capabilities or to design sophisticated input systems.
Pattern of Components:
The Component pattern is a fundamental idea in Unity. GameObjects are composed of components that can be added, removed, or combined to produce a variety of behaviors and functionalities.
State Machine Design:
State machines are used to specify a set of states, their transitions, and the actions or behaviors associated with each state. State machines are commonly used in Unity for character AI, animations, and game flow.
The Builder pattern separates the construction and representation of a complex item. It's handy for generating objects with several optional parameters, making object initialization more readable and versatile.
The Decorator pattern lets you to dynamically provide new responsibilities to an object. This can be used in Unity to change or extend the behavior of components and game objects at runtime.
MVC is a software architecture pattern that divides an application into three interconnected components: the Model (data and business logic), the View (presentation and user interface), and the Controller (which manages user input and communicates between the Model and the View). The MVVM (Model-View-ViewModel) design is frequently used in Unity game development.
Understanding and implementing these scripting patterns in your Unity projects can result in cleaner, more modular, and easier-to-maintain code. Each pattern has a unique purpose and can be customized to meet your game development requirements.

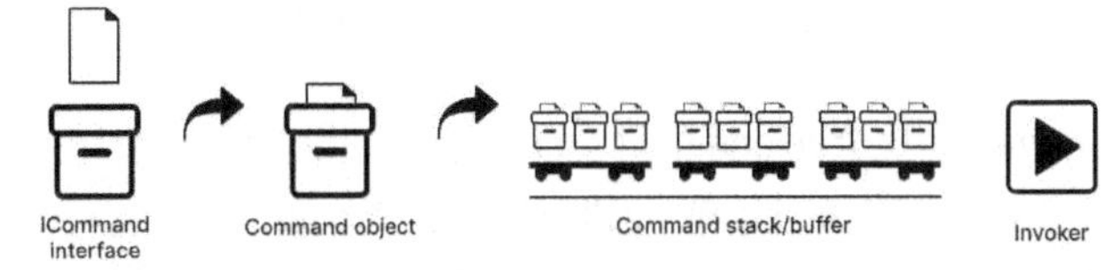

Singletons:

The Singleton design pattern assures that a class only has one instance and gives a global point of access to that instance. It is often used in Unity game development to construct a single, global manager or controller for duties such as managing game settings, coordinating resource loading, or maintaining a central data store.

- Single Instance: The Singleton pattern's key principle is that a class should have only one instance throughout the application's runtime. This avoids the creation of duplicate instances, which could cause confusion or conflicts in your code.
- Global Access: The Singleton allows you to access its one instance from anywhere in your code base. This means you may use it to store and manage data or functionality that should be available across your game without having to explicitly transfer references to it.
- Private Constructor: To enforce the single-instance constraint, the Singleton class often has a private constructor, which means it cannot be constructed from outside code. This ensures that all instances of the class are created and controlled entirely within the class.
- Static Instance: A static instance of the class is created within the Singleton class. This instance is unique and can be obtained by a public static method called "Instance" or "GetSingleton," which returns the single instance.

Here's a simple example of a Singleton in Unity:

```
public class GameManager : MonoBehaviour
{
    private static GameManager instance;

    // Private constructor to prevent external instantiation
    private GameManager() { }

    // Static method to get the single instance
    public static GameManager Instance
    {
        get
        {
            if (instance == null)
            {
                instance = new GameManager();
            }
            return instance;
        }
    }

    // Other game-related methods and properties
    public int Score { get; set; }
}
```

In this example, the GameManager class in this example ensures that there is only one instance of the GameManager throughout the game. GameManager provides access to the GameManager's properties and methods.Instance.

In Unity, the Singleton pattern can be useful for managing global game state, tracking high scores, controlling game settings, or handling any other global activity that should have a single point of access and control. Just be careful not to abuse Singletons because they can make your code less modular and more difficult to test. It's advisable to save them for cases where a single global instance is truly required.

Factory Pattern:

The Factory Pattern is a creational design pattern that provides an interface for creating objects while allowing subclasses to change the type of objects created. The Factory Pattern is extensively used in Unity game development and software engineering in general to centralize and encapsulate object generation, making it easier to manage and grow the codebase. A more extensive explanation of the Factory Pattern in Unity may be found here:

- Separation of Object Creation: The Factory Pattern separates the process of creating objects from the client code that uses those objects. This means that the client code does not need to know the details of how objects are created; it simply requests an object from the factory.
- Abstract Factory and Concrete Factory: The Factory Pattern frequently employs an abstract factory interface or base class that provides a method for object creation. Concrete factories that implement this interface provide specialized object creation implementations. Factorys in Unity can be built as components, scripts, or classes.
- Product Classes: The objects produced by the factory are known as "products." These are the classes that the factory is in charge of creating. Product classes in Unity can represent many types of game objects, components, or other assets.
- Client Code: The client code, which can be located anywhere in your game, communicates with the factory by requesting objects. The client code does not need to know how the objects are formed or which classes are utilized; it depends on the factory to supply the objects.
- Flexibility and Extensibility: The Factory Pattern is adaptable and expandable. If you need to create new sorts of objects or change the way they are formed, just establish a new factory or edit an existing one without changing the client code.

Here's a simplified example of a Factory Pattern in Unity:

```
public abstract class GameObjectFactory
{
    public abstract GameObject CreateGameObject();
}

public class CubeFactory : GameObjectFactory
{
    public override GameObject CreateGameObject()
    {
        return GameObject.CreatePrimitive(PrimitiveType.Cube);
    }
}

public class SphereFactory : GameObjectFactory
{
    public override GameObject CreateGameObject()
    {
        return GameObject.CreatePrimitive(PrimitiveType.Sphere);
    }
}
```

In this case, GameObjectFactory is an abstract factory class containing a method for constructing game objects. CubeFactory and SphereFactory are concrete factory classes that provide unique implementations for constructing cube and sphere game objects. Client code can utilize these factories to produce things without knowing how the objects are created:

```
var cube = new CubeFactory().CreateGameObject();
var sphere = new SphereFactory().CreateGameObject();
```

When dealing with object instantiation, such as creating opponents, power-ups, or other game items, the Factory Pattern is extremely handy with Unity. It encourages code reuse and aids in the management of object generation complexity.
Observer Pattern:

The Observer Pattern is a behavioral design pattern that specifies a one-to-many dependency between objects such that when one object (the subject) changes its state, all of its dependents (observers) are immediately notified and updated. This paradigm is used in Unity game development to construct event handling systems, when numerous components or systems must react to changes in a centralized object without knowing the specifics of what changed. In Unity, here's a more extensive explanation of the Observer Pattern:

- Subject: The "subject" is the core entity that keeps track of its observers and their subscriptions. This can be a game object, a script, or a system with data or state changes that must be transmitted to others in Unity.
- Observer: The "observers" are items or components that show an interest in the subject's status and wish to be notified when it changes. Typically, observers implement an interface or derive from a base class that allows them to receive update notifications.
- Registration and Deregistration: Observers register for the subject, expressing their want to be notified of changes. If they are no longer interested, they can also deregister. This registration process is frequently done in Unity using methods such as "Subscribe" and "Unsubscribe."
- Notification: When the subject's state changes, it calls a method or triggers an event to notify all registered observers. This message may contain data or information regarding the change, allowing observers to respond appropriately.
- Loose Coupling: The Observer Pattern encourages the topic and its observers to be loosely coupled. Observers do not need to understand the minutiae of the subject's implementation; they simply need to comprehend the notification interface or contract.
- Multiple Observers: The subject may have several observers, and each observer may respond differently to the identical change in the subject. This makes it appropriate for applications requiring various components or systems to respond to events.

Subject in this example keeps a list of observers and alerts them when NotifyObservers is called. To define the behavior when receiving updates, ConcreteObserver implements the IObserver interface.
The Observer Pattern can be used in Unity for a variety of applications, including handling player input events, controlling UI updates, and developing custom event systems. It encourages decoupling and makes it easy to extend and modify your game systems' behavior without affecting other portions of the code.

Command Pattern:

The Command Pattern is a behavioral design pattern that encapsulates a request as an object, allowing for request parameterization, request queuing, and request logging. It decouples the sender and recipient of a request, allowing you to parameterize objects with operations and delay request execution. The Command Pattern is important in Unity game development and software engineering for implementing undo/redo capabilities, developing sophisticated input systems, and more. Here's a more extensive explanation of the Unity Command Pattern:

- Command Interface: The Command Pattern starts with an abstract command interface or class that defines a method (usually named Execute) for executing the command. This interface is implemented by concrete command classes.
- Concrete Commands: Concrete command classes implement the command interface. Each concrete command represents a specific action or operation that the client wants to perform. In Unity, these operations can include things like moving a character, firing a weapon, or changing a game state.
- Client: The client is in charge of developing and configuring commands. It determines which commands to run and when to run them. The client may also keep a history of instructions executed, which is useful for implementing undo/redo capabilities.
- Invoker: The invoker is in charge of carrying out the commands. It keeps track of the command objects and calls their Execute methods as needed. In Unity, the invoker can be a game manager, an input manager, or any other system that initiates game operations.
- Receiver: The object that does the real work connected with the command is known as the receiver. To perform the required action, the concrete command classes encapsulate the receiver and invoke the receiver's methods.
- Parameterization: Commands can be parameterized, allowing clients to configure the commands with data. This flexibility makes it possible to reuse command objects with different parameters.
- Undo/Redo: Because instructions encapsulate activities, providing undo/redo capability is simple. You can simply rollback activities by calling the commands in reverse order if you keep a history of executed commands.

Here's a simplified example of the Command Pattern in Unity:

The MoveCommand class in this example represents a command to move a Unity Transform to a defined location. The InputManager is the invoker in charge of carrying out the command when it is activated by player input.

```
// Command interface
public interface ICommand
{
    void Execute();
}

// Concrete command
public class MoveCommand : ICommand
{
    private Transform target;
    private Vector3 destination;

    public MoveCommand(Transform target, Vector3 destination)
    {
        this.target = target;
        this.destination = destination;
    }

    public void Execute()
    {
        target.position = destination;
    }
}

// Invoker
public class InputManager
{
    private ICommand command;

    public void SetCommand(ICommand command)
    {
        this.command = command;
    }

    public void ExecuteCommand()
    {
        if (command != null)
        {
            command.Execute();
        }
    }
}
```

The Unity Command Pattern enables versatile and extensible systems such as custom input processing, AI behavior management, and sophisticated game dynamics that require actions to be encapsulated and performed at precise moments.

Component Pattern:

The Component Pattern is a design pattern that focuses on item organization and composition by dividing them into smaller, reusable components. This pattern is a crucial notion in Unity game creation. To develop complicated behaviors and features, game objects are formed by merging numerous components. A more extensive explanation of the Component Pattern in Unity may be found here:

- Game Objects: A game object is a fundamental building piece in Unity that represents an entity in your scene. In your game, game objects might be anything from people and adversaries to items and scenery.
- Components: Components are self-contained, tiny chunks of functionality that can be connected to game objects. Transform (for position and rotation), Renderer (for generating visuals), Collider (for collision detection), and Script (for custom behavior) are some Unity components.
- Composition: The Component Pattern places a emphasizes on composition over inheritance. You build game objects by attaching diverse components rather than developing big, monolithic classes. This method provides better flexibility and reusability.
- Extensibility: Custom components produced by you or offered by Unity's ecosystem and third-party assets can be added to game objects in Unity. This flexibility allows you to modify and improve game elements as needed for your project.
- Modularity: Components promote modularity in your game's design. Each component can focus on a specific aspect of functionality, making it easier to develop, test, and maintain your game.
- Communication: Interfaces or events allow components to communicate with one another. A custom script component, for example, may connect with a physics component to respond to collisions or with an animation component to initiate animations.
- Reusability: Components are reusable across several game elements. For example, you can reuse the same script component in your game for several characters, avoiding redundancy and code duplication.
- Hierarchy and Nesting: The parent-child connection can be created by layering objects within one another in Unity's game object hierarchy. Components on parent objects can influence their offspring, allowing for complicated interactions and behaviors.
- Inspector: Unity includes an Inspector interface that allows you to visually add, configure, and delete components from game objects.

Here's a simplified example of the Component Pattern in Unity:

We'll make a game object out of numerous components that represents a moving character. For position, we'll use a Transform component, a Rigidbody for physics, and a custom script component for character control.

1. Create a new Unity project if you don't have one already.
2. In the Unity Hierarchy window, right-click and create a 3D Cube. This will be our game object
3. Select the Cube in the Hierarchy. In the Inspector, click "Add Component" and search for "Rigidbody." Add the Rigidbody component. This component will handle physics for our character.
4. In the Project window, create a C# script named "CharacterController".
5. Double-click the "CharacterController" script to open it in your preferred code editor.

```
public class CharacterController : MonoBehaviour
{
    public float moveSpeed = 5f;

    private Rigidbody rb;

    private void Start()
    {
        rb = GetComponent<Rigidbody>();
    }

    private void Update()
    {
        // Get input from arrow keys or WASD
        float moveX = Input.GetAxis("Horizontal");
        float moveZ = Input.GetAxis("Vertical");

        // Calculate movement vector
        Vector3 moveDirection = new Vector3(moveX, 0, moveZ).normalized;

        // Apply force to move the character
        rb.AddForce(moveDirection * moveSpeed);
    }
}
```

This script makes the character to move in response to keyboard input. It uses the Rigidbody component to connect with physics and calculates the character's movement based on input.

In this example, we utilized the Component Pattern to create a game object (the Cube) that is made up of several components, including a Transform, a Rigidbody, and a custom script (CharacterController). Each component contributes to the behavior and functionality of the character, showcasing how Unity's component-based architecture promotes modularity and flexible game object building.

State machine pattern:

The State Machine Pattern is a behavioral design pattern that enables an object's behavior to change when its internal state changes. State machines are frequently used in game development, including Unity, to manage complex and dynamic behaviors of characters, game elements, and systems. A more extensive explanation of the State Machine Pattern in Unity may be found here:

- States: In the State Machine Pattern, a "state" represents a specific condition or mode in which an object can exist. Each state encapsulates a particular set of behaviors, actions, or rules that apply when the object is in that state. States can be things like "idle," "walking," "attacking," or "jumping."
- State Machine: The "state machine" is an object that controls the transition between different states of a game object or system. It manages the current state and ensures that the appropriate state-specific behaviors are executed.
- Transitions: Transitions are the conditions or events that cause a state to transition from one to another. When the player taps a movement key, a character may change from a "idle" state to a "walking" state.
- Behavior Encapsulation: A state machine's states encapsulate the activities associated with that state. As a result, the code is more modular, maintainable, and understandable. There's no need to clog a single script with conditional statements; instead, each state has its own logic.
- Flexibility: State machines are extremely malleable. To change or extend the behavior of your game objects or systems, you may quickly add new states or modify existing ones. This is very important when responding to new requirements or features.

- Hierarchical State Machines: Hierarchical State Machines: You can make hierarchical state machines in Unity, where states can have sub-states. Sub-states inherit their parent states' behaviour, but they can also override or extend them. This allows for more complicated and layered behavior.
- Events and Actions: State machines can be programmed to react to events such as button presses, timers, or user input. When switching between states, they can also initiate actions such as animations, music effects, or gameplay events.
- Debugging and Visualization: Unity provides tools to help visualize and debug state machines, making it easier to track the current state and understand state transitions during development.

State machines are frequently used in Unity to govern game AI, manage player input, and define game progression. The State Machine Pattern helps to build more responsive and dynamic game experiences by simplifying complicated behaviors, improving maintainability, and creating more responsive and dynamic game experiences.

```
public class StateMachine : MonoBehaviour
{
    private MonoBehaviour currentState;

    private void Start()
    {
        // Initialize the state machine with the IdleState
        ChangeState(GetComponent<IdleState>());
    }

    private void Update()
    {
        // Update the current state
        currentState.UpdateState();
    }

    public void ChangeState(MonoBehaviour newState)
    {
        // Exit the current state
        if (currentState != null)
            currentState.ExitState();

        // Change to the new state
        currentState = newState;
        currentState.EnterState();
    }
}
```

Builder Pattern:

The Builder Pattern is a creational design pattern that isolates complex object development from their representation, allowing you to build items step by step. It's handy when an object has several configurations and choices and passing them all as parameters in a single constructor would be impracticable. The Builder Pattern in Unity game development can be used to generate complicated game objects or configurations in a more legible and maintained manner. Here's a more in-depth look at the Builder Pattern in Unity, for instance:

- Director: The "director" in the Builder Pattern is in charge of directing the construction process. The director knows what steps to take to generate the final thing and employs a "builder" to do this.
- Builder: The "builder" is in charge of building the thing step by step. It defines methods for configuring the object's separate components or properties.
- Product: The "product" is the complex thing that is being built. It is often the finished product of the builder's construction procedure.
- Fluent Interface: Builders frequently use a "fluent interface," which allows method calls to be chained together for more compact and understandable code.

To review this on code:

```csharp
// Product
public class Character
{
    public string Name { get; set; }
    public int Health { get; set; }
    public int AttackDamage { get; set; }
    public GameObject Weapon { get; set; }

    public void DisplayInfo()
    {
        Debug.Log($"Name: {Name}, Health: {Health}, Attack Damage: {AttackDamage}");
    }
}
```

```csharp
// Builder
public class CharacterBuilder
{
    private Character character = new Character();

    public CharacterBuilder SetName(string name)
    {
        character.Name = name;
        return this;
    }

    public CharacterBuilder SetHealth(int health)
    {
        character.Health = health;
        return this;
    }

    public CharacterBuilder SetAttackDamage(int attackDamage)
    {
        character.AttackDamage = attackDamage;
        return this;
    }

    public CharacterBuilder SetWeapon(GameObject weapon)
    {
        character.Weapon = weapon;
        return this;
    }

    public Character Build()
    {
        return character;
    }
}
```

```csharp
public class CharacterDirector
{
    public Character ConstructWarrior()
    {
        return new CharacterBuilder()
            .SetName("Warrior")
            .SetHealth(100)
            .SetAttackDamage(20)
            .SetWeapon(Resources.Load<GameObject>("Sword")) // Load a Sword prefab from Resources
            .Build();
    }

    public Character ConstructWizard()
    {
        return new CharacterBuilder()
            .SetName("Wizard")
            .SetHealth(80)
            .SetAttackDamage(30)
            .SetWeapon(Resources.Load<GameObject>("Staff")) // Load a Staff prefab from Resources
            .Build();
    }
}

// Usage
public class CharacterCreationExample : MonoBehaviour
{
    private void Start()
    {
        CharacterDirector director = new CharacterDirector();
        Character warrior = director.ConstructWarrior();
        Character wizard = director.ConstructWizard();

        warrior.DisplayInfo();
        wizard.DisplayInfo();
    }
}
```

We have a Character class in this example that represents a character with numerous attributes. The CharacterBuilder class is used to create a Character object step by step, allowing you to customize its name, health, attack damage, and weapon. The CharacterDirector manages the building process and provides techniques for creating certain character kinds.

Using Unity's Builder Pattern, you may design complicated game items or setups in a systematic, clear, and understandable manner. It's very beneficial when working with things that have a lot of different features or configurations.

Decorator Pattern:

The Decorator Pattern is a structural design pattern that allows you to dynamically add new behavior or responsibilities to objects without changing their existing structure. It's especially handy in Unity game development when you need to extend or modify the behavior of game objects or components in a flexible and maintainable manner. A more extensive explanation of the Decorator Pattern in Unity may be found here:

- Components or Objects: In Unity, components and game objects are the building blocks of your game. They provide specific functionality, like rendering, physics, or scripting.
- Base Component or Object: The "base component" or "base object" represents the object's essential functionality that you want to improve or change. This serves as the foundation for interior designers.
- Decorators: Decorators are classes that extend the functionality or behavior of the basic component or object. They implement the same interface as the basic component in order to be interchangeable.
- Composition: The Decorator Pattern's main notion is to layer decorators on top of a basic component or object. This stacking, or composition, is how multiple duties or features are added.
- Dynamic Extension: Decorators can be added and removed dynamically at runtime. You can mix and match decorators to create different combinations of features for your objects.
- Transparency: From the client's perspective, decorators and the base component should be indistinguishable. This transparency means that you can use a decorated object just like the base object.
- Flexibility: The Decorator Pattern is versatile and adaptable. You can add new decorators without altering current code by creating new decorators. This makes it easier to respond to changing requirements and extend game object behavior.
- Consistency: The pattern encourages a consistent interface, making it easy to collaborate with a wide range of decorators and guarantee they all follow the same contract.

A code example for it is as the following:

```
public interface ICharacter
{
    void Attack();
}

// Concrete Component
public class Character : ICharacter
{
    public void Attack()
    {
        Debug.Log("Character attacks with a basic attack.");
    }
}
```

```
// Decorator
public abstract class CharacterDecorator : ICharacter
{
    private ICharacter character;

    public CharacterDecorator(ICharacter character)
    {
        this.character = character;
    }

    public virtual void Attack()
    {
        character.Attack();
    }
}
```

```
public class MagicDecorator : CharacterDecorator
{
    public MagicDecorator(ICharacter character) : base(charact

    public override void Attack()
    {
        base.Attack();
        Debug.Log("Character attacks with magic spells.");
    }
}
```

```
// Concrete Decorators
public class SwordDecorator : CharacterDecorator
{
    public SwordDecorator(ICharacter character) : base(charact

    public override void Attack()
    {
        base.Attack();
        Debug.Log("Character attacks with a sword.");
    }
}

public class MagicDecorator : CharacterDecorator
{
    public MagicDecorator(ICharacter character) : base(charact

    public override void Attack()
    {
```

We have a Character class in this example that implements the ICharacter interface and represents a simple character. We next develop two decorators, SwordDecorator and MagicDecorator, which provide the character new attack behaviors. Decorators modify the basic character's behavior, allowing it to attack with a sword or cast magic spells.

Usage Code:

```
ICharacter character = new Character();
character = new SwordDecorator(character);
character = new MagicDecorator(character);

character.Attack();
```

In Unity, the Decorator Pattern is useful for increasing game object behaviors without affecting their existing code, such as adding visual effects, actions, or other features to characters, enemies, or any other game entities. It increases game development's maintainability and versatility.

MVC pattern:

The Model-View-Controller (MVC) architectural design pattern is widely used in software development, including Unity game development, to divide an application's responsibilities into three interconnected components: the Model, View, and Controller. By clearly outlining the roles and responsibilities of each component, MVC enhances modularity, maintainability, and code structure. A more extensive explanation of the MVC pattern may be found here:

- Model: The Model represents the data, state, and business logic of the application. It is in charge of handling the application's data and responding to data requests. This could be the game's state, player data, or any other data on which the game depends in Unity.
- View: The View is in charge of displaying data from the Model to the user as well as handling user interface (UI) interactions. It shows information and solicits user input. In Unity, this usually refers to the game's visual representation, which includes the GUI, game objects, and UI elements.
- Controller: The Controller functions as a go-between for the Model and the View. It processes user input from the View and interacts with the Model to change data and status. It manages user actions and responds appropriately in the Model and View. The Controller in Unity is frequently associated with user input handling, character controllers, and game mechanics.

- Loose Coupling: The loose connectivity of the components is a basic principle of MVC. Because of this separation, modifications to one component have no effect on the others, making the program more maintainable and extendable.
- Bidirectional Communication: The components communicate with one another, but only inadvertently. The View can query the Model for information, and the Controller can change the Model and modify the View. This bidirectional connection keeps each component focused on its assigned tasks.
- Scalability and Reusability: The MVC pattern promotes scalability and code reuse. While the Model remains unchanged, you can develop new Views or Controllers to adapt to different UIs or game features.
- Testing: Because the Model, View, and Controller are distinct, writing unit tests for each component is simpler, allowing you to test the application's logic and UI independently.
- Unity-Specific Considerations: In Unity, the View frequently contains game object rendering and the user interface, whereas the Controller includes input processing, character controllers, and game-specific logic. Game data, player stats, and other non-visual features of the game could all be included in the Model.

Assume you're making a game with a player character, a health system (Model), a health bar on the screen (View), and a script that manages the player's interactions (Controller).
The Model stores the player's health value and describes how it varies over time and as a result of various game events.
The View displays the health bar on the screen, which reflects the player's current health. It monitors the Model for updates and displays the health value visually.
The Controller responds to player input (for example, taking damage or utilizing healing items), communicates with the Model to update the health, and triggers changes in the View to update the health bar.
As a result, the MVC pattern helps organize the components of your game, making it easier to maintain, modify, and test your Unity project.

Because of the Unity-specific nature of Views and the built-in MonoBehaviour lifecycle, creating a comprehensive MVC structure in Unity might be difficult. However, I can present a basic example to show how the Model, View, and Controller components can be implemented within Unity.

In this example, the Model represents the player's health, the View is a UI Text element displaying the health, and the Controller alters the player's health with buttons.

1. Create a UI Text Object for the View: In your Unity scene, create a UI Text object (GameObject -> UI -> Text) to display the player's health.
2. Create Scripts for the Model, View, and Controller: Create three C# scripts named "HealthModel," "HealthView," and "HealthController"

HealthModel (Model):

```
public class HealthModel : MonoBehaviour
{
    private int health = 100;

    public int GetHealth()
    {
        return health;
    }

    public void SetHealth(int newHealth)
    {
        health = newHealth;
    }
}
```

HealthView (View):

```
public class HealthView : MonoBehaviour
{
    [SerializeField] private Text healthText;
    private HealthModel model;

    private void Start()
    {
        model = GetComponent<HealthModel>();
    }

    private void Update()
    {
        UpdateHealthText();
    }

    private void UpdateHealthText()
    {
        int currentHealth = model.GetHealth();
        healthText.text = "Health: " + currentHealth;
    }
}
```

Attach the "HealthView" script to the UI Text object you created earlier.
HealthController (Controller):

```
public class HealthController : MonoBehaviour
{
    private HealthModel model;

    private void Start()
    {
        model = GetComponent<HealthModel>();
    }

    public void IncreaseHealth(int amount)
    {
        int currentHealth = model.GetHealth();
        model.SetHealth(currentHealth + amount);
    }

    public void DecreaseHealth(int amount)
    {
        int currentHealth = model.GetHealth();
        model.SetHealth(currentHealth - amount);
    }
}
```

Create Buttons to Control Health: Create UI buttons (GameObject -> UI -> Button) in your scene to increase and decrease the player's health. Each button should have the "HealthController" script attached to it.

Wire Up the Buttons: Assign the IncreaseHealth method to the "OnClick" event of the button for increasing health and the DecreaseHealth method to the button for reducing health in the Inspector.

When you run the scene, you'll see a simple health tracking system built with the MVC architecture. The Model (HealthModel) handles the player's health, the View (HealthView) displays it on the UI, and the Controller (HealthController) alters it when the UI buttons are pressed.

While this is a small example, it highlights the fundamental principles of the MVC pattern in Unity, dividing concerns and responsibilities into different components for better code structure and maintainability.

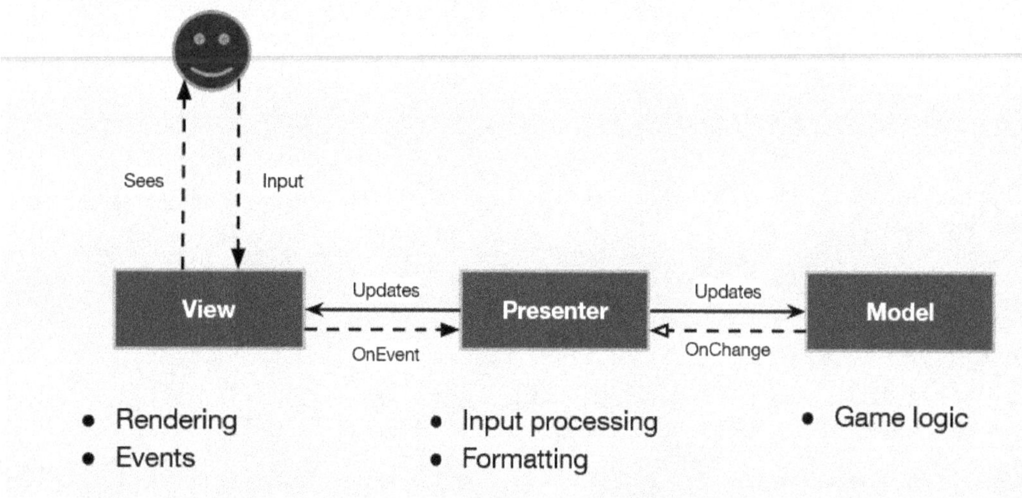

CHAPTER V
[Physics System]

Basic concepts and components :

The physics engine in Unity is a vital component that provides the tools and capability needed to create realistic physical interactions and simulations in your games. It's built on the NVIDIA PhysX engine and integrated into Unity to handle physics-related tasks including collision detection, rigid body dynamics, forces, and more. Here's a more in-depth look at Unity's physics engine:

- Rigidbody and Colliders: The Rigidbody and Collider components form the core of Unity's physics engine. To imitate physical behavior, these components are attached to game objects., a rigidbody component is used to mimic the physical properties of an object, such as mass, gravity, velocity, and angular velocity. It is in charge of simulating dynamic object movement and responding to forces and collisions, a collider specifies the shape and size of a gaming item in order to detect collisions. Box colliders, sphere colliders, capsule colliders, and mesh colliders are among the collider types available in Unity.

- Collision Detection: The collision detection function of Unity's physics engine determines when objects intersect or come into contact. It computes collision sites, normals, and penetration depths to aid in collision response. When collisions occur, Unity includes numerous collision events such as OnCollisionEnter, OnCollisionStay, and OnCollisionExit that allow you to execute custom code.

- Layers and Tags: Objects in Unity can be organized by assigning them to different layers and adding tags. This is important for customizing how objects interact during collision detection.

- Joints and Constraints: The physics engine in Unity contains several joint and constraint components that allow you to connect and constrain objects. These are some examples:
- HingeJoint: This object simulates hinge-like connections.
- FixedJoint: Makes permanent connections between items.
- SpringJoint: Gives connections spring-like action.
- CharacterJoint: This class can be used to simulate character movement and interactions.

- Raycasting: it is a method of detecting collisions and intersections by blasting rays in a specific direction. It's extensively employed for a variety of applications, including character control, shooting mechanics, and object selection.

- Cloth Simulation: Unity includes a Cloth component that can be used to simulate the behavior of fabric and soft bodies. It enables you to simulate realistic cloth and soft objects in your games.

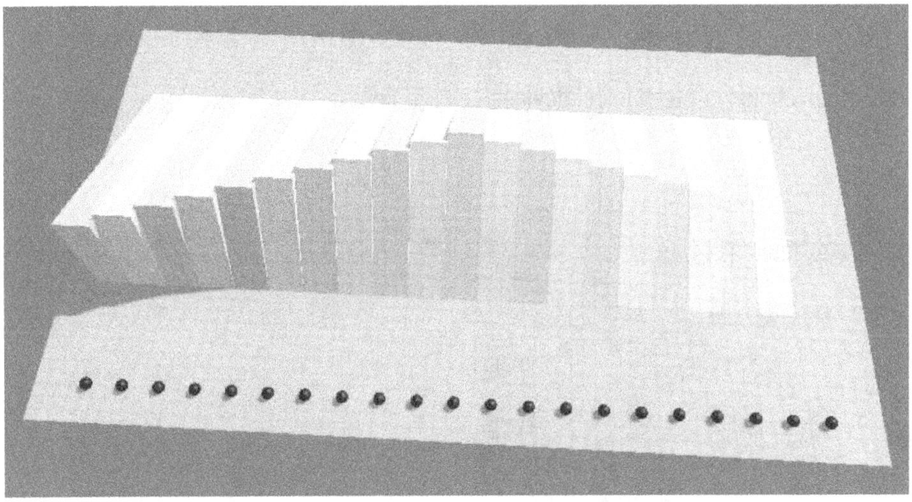

- NavMesh: Unity incorporates the NavMesh system for pathfinding and AI navigation, despite the fact that it is not part of the physics engine itself. It enables players and NPCs to easily travel the game world while avoiding obstacles.

- Optimization and Performance: The physics engine in Unity provides a variety of tools and settings for optimizing efficiency, such as collision layers, trigger colliders (which do not physically interact but trigger events), and physics layers.

- Debugging and Profiling: Unity includes a number of debugging tools and profilers to help you find and fix physics issues in your game. You may visualize physics components and interactions with the Physics Debugger.

- Third-Party Integrations: The physics engine in Unity can be extended and tweaked with third-party plugins and components from the Unity Asset Store. Advanced simulations, fluid dynamics, and other techniques may be used.

Unity's physics engine is essential for producing dynamic and interactive game experiences. By managing physical behaviors and interactions, it enables developers to construct realistic and compelling simulations. Understanding the physics system's concepts and components is critical for creating games with convincing physics-based gameplay and visual effects.

In order to further progress and understand the physics engine a bit more we will study an examples:

we will make a Rube Goldberg Machine:

Within Unity, you will design and create a virtual Rube Goldberg Machine. A Rube Goldberg Machine is a collection of interconnected, over-engineered contraptions that perform a simple task, such as popping a balloon or lighting a candle, in a whimsical and sophisticated manner. Your virtual machine will show off your command of Unity's physics engine.

Features that should be applied to the project in order to work is as the following:

1. User Interface (UI): Create a user-friendly interface that allows users to select various jobs for the Rube Goldberg Machine to execute. Lighting a candle, inflating a balloon, or knocking down a set of dominoes are examples of tasks.
2. Machine Components: Create various components for your Rube Goldberg Machine. These can include things like toppling dominoes.
   Slopes and ramps for rolling items.
   Pendulums that swing back and forth.
   Levers, pulleys, and switches are all examples of mechanical devices.
   Belt conveyors.
   Catapults and springs.
   Fans and blowers of air.
   Balloons, balls, and other things are examples of this.

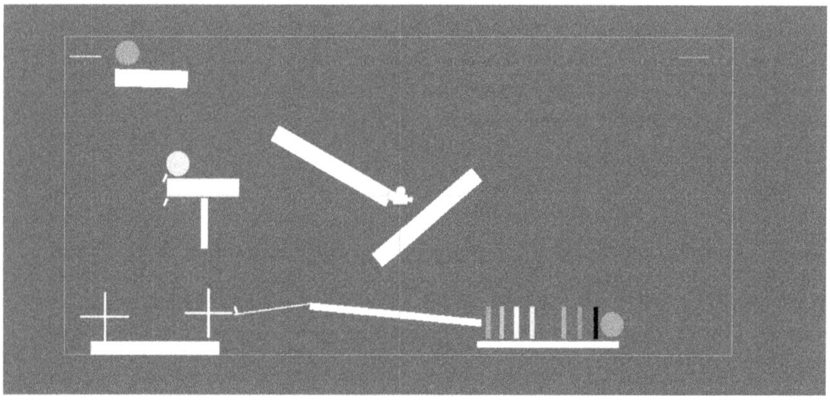

3. Physics Simulation: Implement the physics for each component, making sure they interact realistically. For realistic physical behavior, use Unity's Rigidbody components, Colliders, and Joints.
4. Chaining Events: When triggered, each component should trigger the following component in a chain reaction. A rolling ball, for example, could start a fan that blows a balloon.

5. Animations: To make the machine more visually appealing and amusing, add custom animations to various portions of it.
6. Task Completion: Provide visual and audible feedback to signal success when the machine completes its task. Play a celebration animation and sound effect, for example, if the task is to pop a balloon.
7. Multiple Tasks: Implement various tasks from which users can choose via the UI. Each task should necessitate a distinct sequence of actions in the machine.
8. Sandbox Mode: Allow users to play with the machine by adding, altering, or rearranging components to build their own contraptions.
9. Simulation Controls: Controls for modifying the physics simulation speed, halting, and resetting the machine should be provided.

User Interface (UI):

Creating a user interface (UI) for your Rube Goldberg Machine project is critical for offering user interaction and customization. In this phase, we'll collaborate to design and build a simple user interface for your project. To create the user interface, we'll use Unity's UI tools.

1. Create a Canvas: Right-click in the Hierarchy panel of your Unity project, pick UI, and then "Canvas." This will generate a canvas that will act as the foundation for your user interface.
   Locate the Canvas component in the Inspector window and change its Render Mode to "Screen Space - Overlay." This guarantees that the UI elements are displayed above the game view.
2. Add UI Elements : Right-click the Canvas in the Hierarchy panel, go to UI, and select "Dropdown." This creates a dropdown element. Right-click the Canvas, go to UI, and select "Button". Right-click the Canvas, go to UI, and select "Text." This text element will display the selected task's description.
3. Position and Customize UI Elements: Select the UI elements in the Hierarchy panel and edit their parameters in the Inspector panel to position and personalize them. To match the design of your game, you can change the size, location, font, color, and other visual elements. As an example:

   You can add task alternatives to the dropdown (for example, "Pop a Balloon," "Light a Candle") by opening the Dropdown component in the Inspector and adding items.
   Change the button text to "Start Machine".
   Make the text element for the job description empty at first.
4. Add UI Functionality: Let us now add functionality to the UI elements:
   Dropdown for Task Selection:
   To control task selection, write a C# script. This script should be in charge of modifying the task description text based on the task selected from the dropdown.
   Starting the Machine Button:
   To control the Rube Goldberg Machine, write a C# script. When the button is pressed, the machine should begin doing the designated task. In this script, you must configure the sophisticated machine interactions.
5. Examine Your User Interface: In the Unity editor, test your user interface. Check that picking a task from the menu changes the task description text and that pressing the "Start Machine" button starts the machine's behavior for the specified task.

   Keep in mind that the exact functionality and customisation of your UI will be determined by the specifics of your Rube Goldberg Machine project and the duties you wish to highlight.

This is some code examples:

```
using UnityEngine;
using UnityEngine.UI;
using System.Collections.Generic;

public class TaskSelectionUI : MonoBehaviour
{
    public Text taskDescriptionText;

    private Dropdown taskDropdown;
    private List<string> taskOptions = new List<string>
    {
        "Pop a Balloon",
        "Light a Candle",
        // Add more task options here
    };

    private void Start()
    {
        taskDropdown = GetComponent<Dropdown>();

        // Populate the dropdown with task options
        taskDropdown.ClearOptions();
        taskDropdown.AddOptions(taskOptions);

        // Set a default task
        taskDropdown.value = 0; // Change to the desired default task index
        taskDescriptionText.text = GetTaskDescription(taskDropdown.value);

        // Register a callback to update the task description when a new task is selected
        taskDropdown.onValueChanged.AddListener(OnTaskSelectionChanged);
    }

    private void OnTaskSelectionChanged(int taskIndex)
    {
        taskDescriptionText.text = GetTaskDescription(taskIndex);
    }

    private string GetTaskDescription(int taskIndex)
    {
        // Define descriptions for each task option (customize as needed)
        switch (taskIndex)
        {
            case 0:
                return "Pop a Balloon: Make the machine pop a balloon in a creative way.";
            case 1:
                return "Light a Candle: Use the machine to light a candle in an intricate manner.";
            // Add more task descriptions here
            default:
                return "No task description available.";
        }
    }
}
```

```
using UnityEngine;
using UnityEngine.UI;
using System.Collections.Generic;

public class MachineControlUI : MonoBehaviour
{
    public Dropdown taskDropdown;
    public Text taskDescriptionText;

    private void Start()
    {
        Button button = GetComponent<Button>();

        // Register a callback for the button's click event
        button.onClick.AddListener(StartMachine);
    }

    private void StartMachine()
    {
        // Get the selected task from the dropdown
        int selectedTaskIndex = taskDropdown.value;
        string selectedTask = taskDropdown.options[selectedTaskIndex].text;

        // You can implement the Rube Goldberg Machine logic here for the selected task
        // This is where the complex physics interactions and animations should be set up

        // Update the task description text
        taskDescriptionText.text = "Machine is in progress: " + selectedTask;
    }
}
```

Attach the TaskSelectionUI script to the Dropdown UI element and use the Inspector to attach it to the Text UI element where you want to show task descriptions.

Attach the MachineControlUI script to the UI element Button. Link the taskDropdown field in the Inspector to the Dropdown UI element for task selection, and the taskDescriptionText field to the Text UI element for displaying the current task description.

The MachineControlUI script's StartMachine method serves as a placeholder for the actual machine's behavior. You should replace this with the logic from your Rube Goldberg Machine.

You can edit the task descriptions in the TaskSelectionUI script's GetTaskDescription method to match the tasks you wish to highlight in your project.

In your Rube Goldberg Machine project's UI, this code provides a basic structure for job selection and machine activation. As part of your project's logic, you will need to develop the sophisticated physics and animations that correspond to each task.

Machine Components:

Making the machine components for your Rube Goldberg Machine may be a creative and exciting task. Each component should interact or behave in a unique way that adds to the chain reaction. Here's a simple demonstration of how to make and script two machine components in Unity: a swinging pendulum and a rolling ball.

Creating the Pendulum:

1. Create a new empty GameObject in your scene to serve as the pendulum's pivot point. This GameObject will represent the pendulum's upper anchor.
2. Make a 3D object to represent the pendulum arm (e.g., a Cube or Cylinder). It can be resized and positioned as needed.
3. To indicate the pivot point for the pendulum's bob, create an empty GameObject (an empty child of the pendulum arm).
4. As the pendulum bobs, make a 3D object (e.g., a Sphere). This item should be a child of the pivot point of the pendulum arm.
5. Connect the pendulum bob to a HingeJoint component. Set the axis of rotation and configure it with the pivot point of the pendulum arm as the connected body.
6. To control the motion of the pendulum, write a C# script (e.g., "Pendulum.cs"). This script should be attached to the pendulum arm.

```
using UnityEngine;

public class Pendulum : MonoBehaviour
{
    public float swingForce = 5.0f;

    private HingeJoint hinge;
    private Rigidbody rb;

    private void Start()
    {
        hinge = GetComponent<HingeJoint>();
        rb = hinge.connectedBody;

        // Apply an initial force to start the pendulum swinging
        rb.AddForce(Vector3.right * swingForce, ForceMode.Impulse);
    }
}
```

Creating the Rolling Ball:

To depict the rolling ball, create a new 3D object (e.g., a Sphere). Place it at an appropriate beginning position.

Connect the rolling ball to a Rigidbody component. This enables it to react to physical forces.

To control the ball's motion, write a C# script (e.g., "RollingBall.cs"). This script should be attached to the rolling ball.

```
using UnityEngine;

public class RollingBall : MonoBehaviour
{
    public float rollForce = 10.0f;

    private Rigidbody rb;

    private void Start()
    {
        rb = GetComponent<Rigidbody>();

        // Apply an initial force to start the ball rolling
        rb.AddForce(Vector3.forward * rollForce, ForceMode.Impulse);
    }
}
```

Interaction and Triggering:

To start a chain reaction, make the swinging motion of the pendulum trigger the motion of the rolling ball. A trigger collider on the pendulum bob can be used to detect when it swings into contact with the ball. When the ball collides, you can impart a force to it to set it in motion.

As a trigger for the pendulum bob, add a Collider (e.g., Sphere Collider). This collider should be large enough to collide with the rolling ball when it is swinging.

Create an OnTriggerEnter method in the Pendulum.cs script to detect the collision with the rolling ball and apply a force to it.

```
void OnTriggerEnter(Collider other)
{
    if (other.CompareTag("Ball")) // Assuming you've tagged the rolling ball as "Ball"
    {
        // Apply a force to the rolling ball to set it in motion
        other.GetComponent<Rigidbody>().AddForce(Vector3.forward * rollForce, ForceMode.Impulse);
    }
}
```

Testing and results:
When you press the Play button in Unity, the pendulum should swing, causing the rolling ball to begin rolling. This is a basic example of how to configure machine components and interactions in your Rube Goldberg Machine project.

You can keep adding components, interactions, and custom scripts to make a complex and fascinating chain reaction. Each machine component should interact with the next in the chain, resulting in a compelling and amusing Rube Goldberg Machine.

Physics Simulation:

It takes several steps to create the physics simulation for your Rube Goldberg Machine. Set up Rigidbody components, colliders, and custom scripts to control and trigger events to replicate the chain reaction and interactions between various machine components. In this example, we'll show how to imitate the swing of a pendulum by activating a rolling ball.

Step 1: Make a Pendulum Setup

To begin, ensure that you have completed the preceding steps to establish the pendulum setup with the "Pendulum" script attached to the pendulum arm. The "Pendulum" script applies an initial force to begin swinging the pendulum.
Step 2: Construct the Rolling Ball Setup

Assemble the rolling ball with a Rigidbody component and the "RollingBall" script.

When the scene begins, an initial force is applied to the ball in the Start method of the "RollingBall" script to get it rolling.

Step 3: Interaction with the Trigger

You'll need to add a trigger collider on the pendulum bob and handle the collision event in the pendulum script to create the interaction where the pendulum's bob triggers the rolling ball.

```
public class Pendulum : MonoBehaviour
{
    public float swingForce = 5.0f;
    public Rigidbody ballRigidbody; // Reference to the ball's Rigidbody

    private HingeJoint hinge;
    private Rigidbody rb;
    private bool triggered = false; // A flag to track if the pendulum has triggered the ball

    private void Start()
    {
        hinge = GetComponent<HingeJoint>();
        rb = hinge.connectedBody;

        // Apply an initial force to start the pendulum swinging
        rb.AddForce(Vector3.right * swingForce, ForceMode.Impulse);
    }

    private void Update()
    {
        if (!triggered)
        {
            // Check if the pendulum has swung to a certain angle (e.g., -45 degrees)
            if (transform.localRotation.eulerAngles.z < -45f)
            {
                TriggerBall();
            }
        }
    }

    private void TriggerBall()
    {
        // Apply a force to the ball to set it in motion
        ballRigidbody.AddForce(Vector3.forward * swingForce, ForceMode.Impulse);
        triggered = true; // Set the trigger flag to prevent further triggering
    }
}
```

Connect the Ball's Rigidbody:

Select the pendulum arm GameObject in the Unity editor, and in the Inspector, you'll find a field for the "Ball Rigidbody." Drag and drop the rolling ball's Rigidbody component into this field.

Include a Trigger Collider:

In the Hierarchy panel, choose the pendulum bob GameObject. To make it a trigger collider, add a Sphere Collider component and tick the "Is Trigger" checkbox. Adjust the trigger collider's size and position such that it encompasses the area where the pendulum will collide with the ball.

With these modifications, the pendulum will cause the rolling ball to begin rolling when it swings to a specific angle. You can extend this interaction by adding more machine components and scripts to your Rube Goldberg Machine to build a longer and more intricate chain reaction.

Chaining Events:

In your Rube Goldberg Machine, chaining events entails developing a series of interactions in which one component activates the next component in the chain. We've previously built up the interaction in which the pendulum causes the rolling ball to move. Let us now extend this idea to include other machine components and interactions.

Step 1: Create Additional Machine Components

Create the additional machine components that will be part of your chain reaction first. You can, for example, include a see-saw, a domino system, and a lever.

Make the necessary GameObjects and 3D models for these components.
Attach the essential components to each of them, such as Rigidbody components for moving or rotating objects.
To manage the behavior of each component, write individual scripts for each one. When a given condition is met, the logic in these scripts should trigger the next component in the sequence.

Step 2: Create a Trigger Mechanism

A trigger mechanism is required to chain the occurrences. In your situation, the pendulum will set off the chain reaction. The TriggerBall method in the pendulum's script is used to start the rolling ball's motion.

This script can be expanded to incorporate the activation of other components. For example, you could write a method called TriggerSeeSaw that tilts the see-saw and then triggers something else.

To demonstrate this principle, inside the pendulum script we made before will make the following changes:

```csharp
public class Pendulum : MonoBehaviour
{
    public float swingForce = 5.0f;
    public Rigidbody ballRigidbody; // Reference to the ball's Rigidbody
    public GameObject seeSaw; // Reference to the see-saw GameObject

    private HingeJoint hinge;
    private Rigidbody rb;
    private bool triggered = false; // A flag to track if the pendulum has triggered the ball

    private void Start()
    {
        hinge = GetComponent<HingeJoint>();
        rb = hinge.connectedBody;

        // Apply an initial force to start the pendulum swinging
        rb.AddForce(Vector3.right * swingForce, ForceMode.Impulse);
    }

    private void Update()
    {
        if (!triggered)
        {
            // Check if the pendulum has swung to a certain angle (e.g., -45 degrees)
            if (transform.localRotation.eulerAngles.z < -45f)
            {
                TriggerBall();
                TriggerSeeSaw(); // Add a call to trigger the see-saw
            }
        }
    }

    private void TriggerBall()
    {
        // Apply a force to the ball to set it in motion
        ballRigidbody.AddForce(Vector3.forward * swingForce, ForceMode.Impulse);
        triggered = true; // Set the trigger flag to prevent further triggering
    }

    private void TriggerSeeSaw()
    {
        // Add logic to tilt the see-saw or trigger another event here
        // For example, you can use the see-saw's Rigidbody to apply a force and make it tilt.
    }
}
```

Step 3: Repetition of the Procedure

Repeat for each component of your Rube Goldberg Machine. The script for each component should provide a method for triggering the next event, which could be the activation of another machine component, the launch of an item, or any other creative interaction you develop.
You can make your Rube Goldberg Machine progressively trigger numerous components, eventually resulting to the intended consequence or task, such as popping a balloon or lighting a candle, by generating this chain of events. To make the machine fun and whimsical, be imaginative and experiment with different interactions and effects for each component.

Pendulum Animation:

Adding unique animations to your Rube Goldberg Machine in Unity can improve its visual appeal and make it more interesting. In this example, we'll make a bespoke animation for your machine's pendulum and rolling ball. To create the animations, we'll use Unity's Animator.
Step 1: Create Pendulum Animation

In the Hierarchy panel, choose the pendulum arm GameObject.

Click the "Add Component" button in the Inspector and search for "Animator." To the pendulum arm, add the Animator component.

By right-clicking in the Assets panel and selecting Create -> Animator Controller, you may create a new Animation Controller. Give it the name "PendulumAnimation."

To open the Animator window, double-click the "PendulumAnimation" icon.

Create two animation states in the Animator window: "Swinging" and "Idle."

To create states, right-click in the Animator window and select "Create State" -> "Empty".
Right-click a state to make it the default.
Drag from one state to another to connect transitions between them.
Select the "Swinging" state, then click the "Add Behaviour" button in the Inspector and select "Script." Attach a C# script (for example, "PendulumAnimation.cs") that controls the animation.

```
public class PendulumAnimation : StateMachineBehaviour
{
    public float swingSpeed = 60.0f;

    private Transform pendulumTransform;

    override public void OnStateEnter(Animator animator, AnimatorStateInfo stateInfo, int layerIndex)
    {
        pendulumTransform = animator.gameObject.transform;
    }

    override public void OnStateUpdate(Animator animator, AnimatorStateInfo stateInfo, int layerIndex)
    {
        pendulumTransform.localRotation = Quaternion.Euler(0f, 0f, Mathf.Sin(Time.time * swingSpeed) * 45f);
    }
}
```

Create a transition from the "Swinging" state to the "Idle" state. Set the criteria of the transition (for example, "Exit Time" or a parameter) to control when the pendulum stops swinging.

To begin the animation, add an event to the "Pendulum" script that initiates the transition from "Idle" to "Swinging." When the pendulum, for example, triggers the ball, it can also start this animation event.

Step 2: Make a Ball Animation

In the Hierarchy panel, choose the rolling ball GameObject.

Incorporate an Animator component into the rolling ball.

Make an Animation Controller (for example, "BallAnimation").

For the rolling ball, open the Animator window.
Make two different animation states: "Rolling" and "Idle."

Select the "Rolling" state and add a C# script (e.g., "RollingBallAnimation.cs") to the Inspector to control the ball's movement during animation.

```
public class RollingBallAnimation : StateMachineBehaviour
{
    public float rollSpeed = 5.0f;

    private Rigidbody ballRigidbody;

    override public void OnStateEnter(Animator animator, AnimatorStateInfo stateInfo, int layerIndex)
    {
        ballRigidbody = animator.gameObject.GetComponent<Rigidbody>();
        ballRigidbody.isKinematic = false;
        ballRigidbody.AddForce(Vector3.forward * rollSpeed, ForceMode.VelocityChange);
    }
}
```

Make a change from "Idle" to "Rolling."
To start the animation, use the same event in the "Pendulum" script that starts the ball moving.

Step 3: Set Up Events and Transitions

Create a system in your scripts (for example, "Pendulum.cs" and "RollingBall.cs") to start the animation events when you want them to. This could happen when the pendulum reaches a certain angle or interacts with another component.

To activate the pendulum animation, for example, add the following code to the "Pendulum.cs" script:

```
void TriggerPendulumAnimation()
{
    // Trigger the "Swinging" animation
    animator.SetBool("IsSwinging", true);
}
```

Add a similar method to the "RollingBall.cs" script to initiate the ball's animation when the moment is correct.

To obtain the desired visual effect, remember to define animation transitions, conditions, and timing within the Animator window.

You may design bespoke animations for the pendulum and rolling ball by following these steps, and you can extend this method to other machine components in your Rube Goldberg Machine. As your machine begins its chain reaction, the animations will make it more aesthetically appealing and fascinating to watch.

Task Completion:

The final and most fulfilling aspect of the procedure is completing a task in your Rube Goldberg Machine. You can add feedback to signify the task's accomplishment when the machine successfully completes its chain reaction. Let's go over how to make a simple task completion feedback in Unity.

Step 1: Create Task Completion Objects

Create completion objects or effects for tasks. You can, for example, make a 3D model of a popped balloon, a lit candle, or any other object relevant to your assignment. Place these objects where they should go when the task is finished. Make sure the task completion objects are dormant or invisible at first.

Step 2: Modify Scripts
You'll need to add logic to your scripts (e.g., "Pendulum.cs" or other related scripts) to trigger the task completion and activate the linked objects. Let's use the pendulum example to finish a task.

```
public class Pendulum : MonoBehaviour
{
    public float swingForce = 5.0f;
    public GameObject balloon; // Reference to the balloon GameObject

    private HingeJoint hinge;
    private Rigidbody rb;
    private bool triggered = false;

    private void Start()
    {
        hinge = GetComponent<HingeJoint>();
        rb = hinge.connectedBody;
        balloon.SetActive(false); // Ensure the balloon is initially inactive
        // Apply an initial force to start the pendulum swinging
        rb.AddForce(Vector3.right * swingForce, ForceMode.Impulse);
    }

    private void Update()
    {
        if (!triggered)
        {
            // Check if the pendulum has swung to a certain angle (e.g., -45 degrees)
            if (transform.localRotation.eulerAngles.z < -45f)
            {
                TriggerBalloon(); // Trigger task completion
            }
        }
    }

    private void TriggerBalloon()
    {
        // Activate the balloon to show it has popped
        balloon.SetActive(true);
        triggered = true; // Set the trigger flag to prevent further triggering
    }
}
```

Step 3: Set Up Task Completion Animation (Optional)

To make the job completion object more aesthetically appealing, you might add a simple animation. Set up an Animator for the task completion object using the steps in the "Create Custom Animations" section.

Step 4: Testing and Evaluation

In Unity, press the Play button to put your Rube Goldberg Machine to the test. When the pendulum initiates the task (for example, popping a balloon), the relevant objects (for example, a popped balloon) should display in the scene.

You can additionally enhance the task completion experience by adding audio effects, particles, or other visual feedback.

When the Rube Goldberg Machine successfully completes its work, you can feel a sense of satisfaction and entertainment by following these steps. You can tailor the task completion feedback to the precise task you wish to highlight in your project.

Multiple Tasks:

Including many tasks in your Rube Goldberg Machine project increases the experience's variety and complexity. Each task can have its own interaction sequence and custom components. In this section, we'll go through how to set up several jobs in Unity with user-selectable settings.

Step 1: Task Selection UI

Follow the methods outlined earlier to develop a UI where users can choose from a variety of tasks. This user interface should have a dropdown selection of task alternatives (for example, "Pop a Balloon," "Light a Candle") as well as a button to start the machine.

To represent each task completion object or effect, create a GameObject. You can, for example, identify each activity with a balloon, a candle, or any other thing.
Make sure that these task completion objects are dormant or invisible at first.

Step 2: Modify Scripts

You must alter your existing scripts (e.g., "Pendulum.cs" or any appropriate scripts) to handle multiple tasks. Here's an

Step 3: Task Selection Functionality

To change the selected task based on the user's decision, call the SetSelectedTask method in the "Pendulum.cs" script in your UI scripts. Here's how to change the UI script (for example, "TaskSelectionUI.cs") to set the selected task:

```csharp
public class TaskSelectionUI : MonoBehaviour
{
    public Text taskDescriptionText;
    public Pendulum pendulum; // Reference to the Pendulum script

    private Dropdown taskDropdown;
    private List<string> taskOptions = new List<string>
    {
        "Pop a Balloon",
        "Light a Candle",
        // Add more task options here
    };

    private void Start()
    {
        taskDropdown = GetComponent<Dropdown>();

        // Populate the dropdown with task options
        taskDropdown.ClearOptions();
        taskDropdown.AddOptions(taskOptions);

        // Set a default task
        taskDropdown.value = 0; // Change to the desired default task index
        taskDescriptionText.text = GetTaskDescription(taskDropdown.value);

        // Register a callback to update the task description and selected task
        taskDropdown.onValueChanged.AddListener(OnTaskSelectionChanged);
    }

    private void OnTaskSelectionChanged(int taskIndex)
    {
        taskDescriptionText.text = GetTaskDescription(taskIndex);
        pendulum.SetSelectedTask(taskIndex); // Update the selected task in the Pendulum script
    }

    private string GetTaskDescription(int taskIndex)
    {
        // Define descriptions for each task option (customize as needed)
        switch (taskIndex)
        {
            case 0:
                return "Pop a Balloon: Make the machine pop a balloon in a creative way.";
            case 1:
                return "Light a Candle: Use the machine to light a candle in an intricate manner.";
            // Add more task descriptions here
            default:
                return "No task description available.";
        }
    }
}
```

Your Rube Goldberg Machine will now support many tasks, and users can select the desired activity using the dropdown UI. When the task is successfully performed, the appropriate task completion objects (e.g., balloon or candle) will display. This pattern can be extended to handle as many tasks as you desire, each with its own set of interactions and effects.

Sandbox Mode:

Adding a "Sandbox Mode" to your Rube Goldberg Machine project lets users to engage with it, play with it, and build their own chain reactions. Here's how to make a simple sandbox mode in Unity:

Step 1: Set Up the Environment

In Unity, create a separate scene or section within your existing scene for the sandbox mode. This area should have ample space for users to place and interact with components.

Create a UI panel to toggle between "Sandbox Mode" and "Demo Mode" (where the machine runs automatically).

Step 2: Create and Place Components

Provide a selection of machine components in your sandbox scene that users may drag and drop into the environment. Swinging pendulums, rolling balls, see-saws, dominoes, and any other features you've invented might be included.

Attach scripts to these components to allow the user to move and interact with them. Custom scripts may be required for object placement and manipulation.

Step 3: User Interaction

You can create simple drag-and-drop functionality to allow users to interact with components. Here's an example of a simple drag-and-drop system in action:

```
public class ComponentInteraction : MonoBehaviour
{
    private bool isDragging = false;
    private Vector3 offset;
    private Rigidbody rb;

    private void Start()
    {
        rb = GetComponent<Rigidbody>();
    }

    private void OnMouseDown()
    {
        offset = transform.position - Camera.main.ScreenToWorldPoint(Input.mousePosition);
        isDragging = true;
        rb.isKinematic = true;
    }

    private void OnMouseDrag()
    {
        if (isDragging)
        {
            Vector3 curScreenPoint = new Vector3(Input.mousePosition.x, Input.mousePosition.y, offset.z);
            Vector3 curPosition = Camera.main.ScreenToWorldPoint(curScreenPoint);
            transform.position = curPosition;
        }
    }

    private void OnMouseUp()
    {
        isDragging = false;
        rb.isKinematic = false;
    }
}
```

Step 4: Enable Sandbox Mode Toggle

Make a UI button that switches users between "Sandbox Mode" and "Demo Mode." When users engage "Sandbox Mode," they can begin dragging and arranging components in the scene.

Step 5: Testing and Troubleshooting

To confirm that users may interact with and manipulate machine components, test the sandbox mode. Make necessary changes to improve the user experience.

Step 6: Optionally save and load configurations

You can improve the sandbox experience by allowing users to save and load machine configurations. Users can experiment with different setups and return to them later in this manner.

Step 7: Provide Instructions and Tutorials

Consider giving in-game assistance or tutorials to assist users in efficiently using the sandbox mode. Explain how each component works and how they can cause their own chain reactions.

You may build an exciting sandbox mode for your Rube Goldberg Machine project by following these instructions, allowing users to explore and experiment with different interactions and component configurations.

Simulation Controls:

Users can start, pause, reset, and control the simulation by adding simulation controls to your Rube Goldberg Machine project. Here is how to configure simulation controls in Unity:

Step 1: Design UI Elements

Create UI elements for simulation controls in your Unity project. These can contain start, pause, and reset buttons for the simulation.

Other options, such as a slider for altering the simulation speed, are optional.

Step 2: UI Layout

Arrange the UI elements for simulation control on the screen. To design a clean and user-friendly interface, use Unity's UI Canvas and Layout components.

Step 3: Create a Control Script
To control the simulation, write a C# script. This script is responsible for beginning, pausing, resetting, and modifying the simulation speed.

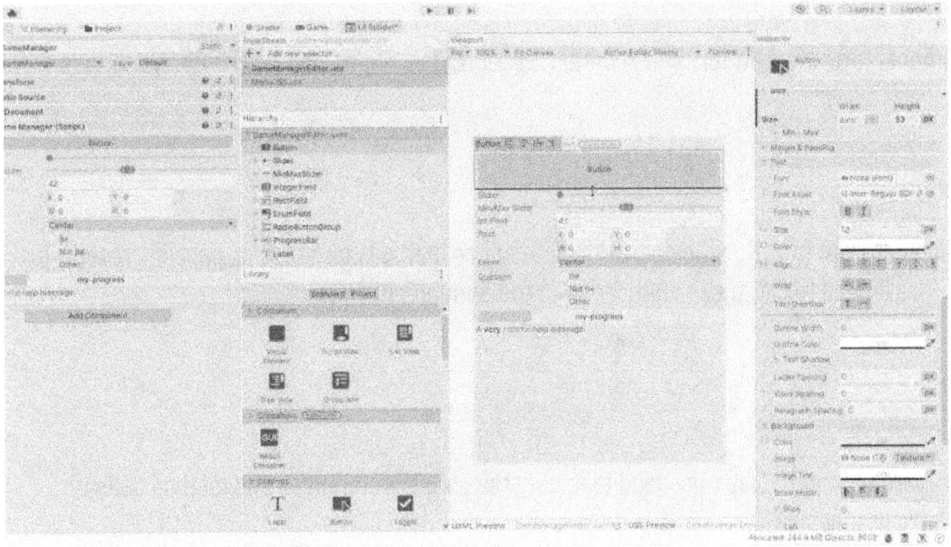

```
using UnityEngine.UI;

public class SimulationControl : MonoBehaviour
{
    public RubeGoldbergMachine machine; // Reference to your machine's script
    public Slider speedSlider; // Optional slider for simulation speed
    public Text speedText; // Optional text to display simulation speed

    private bool isRunning = false;

    private void Start()
    {
        // Set the initial state of controls
        SetControlState();
    }

    public void StartSimulation()
    {
        isRunning = true;
        machine.StartMachine(); // Replace with the appropriate method in your machine script
        SetControlState();
    }

    public void PauseSimulation()
    {
        isRunning = false;
        machine.PauseMachine(); // Replace with the appropriate method in your machine script
        SetControlState();
    }

    public void ResetSimulation()
    {
        isRunning = false;
        machine.ResetMachine(); // Replace with the appropriate method in your machine script
        SetControlState();
    }

    public void AdjustSimulationSpeed()
    {
        float newSpeed = speedSlider.value;
        machine.SetSimulationSpeed(newSpeed); // Replace with the appropriate method in your machine script
        speedText.text = "Speed: " + newSpeed.ToString("F2");
    }

    private void SetControlState()
    {
        // Update button interactivity based on the simulation state
        bool isMachineActive = machine.IsMachineActive(); // Replace with the appropriate method in your machine script
        bool isMachinePaused = machine.IsMachinePaused(); // Replace with the appropriate method in your machine script

        // Enable or disable buttons based on the current state
        startButton.interactable = !isMachineActive;
        pauseButton.interactable = isMachineActive && !isMachinePaused;
        resetButton.interactable = isMachineActive || isMachinePaused;

        // Enable or disable slider and text
        speedSlider.interactable = !isMachineActive;
        speedText.enabled = !isMachineActive;
    }
}
```

Step 4: Attach the Script and UI Elements

In your scenario, attach the SimulationControl script to an empty GameObject.

Drag and drop the necessary UI elements (e.g., Start button, Pause button, Reset button, Slider, and Text) onto the script's public fields in the Unity Inspector.

Step 5: Control Machine Script

Ensure that your Rube Goldberg Machine script (e.g., RubeGoldbergMachine.cs) has methods for starting, pausing, resetting, and adjusting the simulation speed. You'll need to call these methods from the SimulationControl script.

Step 6: Testing and Troubleshooting

Check that the simulation controls operate properly. You may need to modify the scripts' references and method calls to match the structure and operation of your machine.

After completing these steps, you will have a set of simulation controls that will allow users to interact with your Rube Goldberg Machine, start and pause the simulation, reset it, and possibly alter the speed for a more interactive and engaging experience.

There is more details about the unity physics that you can use to make much more unique games like:

1. Physics Layers and Matrix: Unity has a collision matrix that allows you to specify which layers can interact with one another. This is useful for improving performance and avoiding collisions. Go to Edit -> Project Settings -> Physics and configure the Layer Collision Matrix to access and edit the collision matrix.
2. Interpolation and Extrapolation: Interpolation and extrapolation are features of Unity's physics engine that help increase the smoothness and precision of physics-based movement. Interpolation smoothes out objects by mixing locations across frames, whereas extrapolation anticipates item positions beyond the current frame to increase responsiveness.
3. Physics Materials: In Unity, you can develop Physics Materials that influence how objects interact with one another. To precisely imitate diverse surfaces and materials, you can alter factors such as friction and bounciness.
4. Raycasting: Raycasting is a key physics-based interaction tool in Unity. It enables you to send a ray in a specific direction and identify what it collides with. Advanced raycasting techniques include raycasting against specific layers, ignoring triggers, and filtering hits via LayerMasks.
5. CCD (Continuous Collision Detection): CCD prevents fast-moving objects from going through other objects without colliding. You can enable CCD on Rigidbodies to improve the accuracy of interactions between fast-moving objects.
6. Rigidbody Constraints: Rigidbodies can be confined to move only along certain axes. Constraints help to simulate things with limited movement, such as a door that can only swing open along one axis.
7. Rigidbody Interpolation: You can set a Rigidbody's interpolation mode to interpolate its movement between frames. When rendering fast-moving objects, this can help to reduce visual artifacts. Depending on your needs, select Interpolate, Extrapolate, or None.
8. Joints: Unity includes a number of joints for joining Rigidbodies. Hinge Joint, Spring Joint, Fixed Joint, Character Joint, and Configurable Joint are examples of these. Advanced physics interactions frequently require the use of joint combinations to build complicated mechanisms.
9. Custom Physics Layers: In addition to the usual layers, Unity allows you to construct custom physics layers. This is useful when your game contains unique interactions between certain objects or groups of things.

10. Performance Optimization: Advanced physics frequently necessitates performance optimization. To lessen the computational strain of physics calculations, approaches such as object pooling, mesh simplification, and LOD (Level of Detail) systems can be used.
11. Physics Queries: In addition to conventional raycasting, Unity has physics inquiries such as SphereCast, CapsuleCast, and BoxCast, which allow you to cast various shapes to detect collisions and intersections.
12. Multi-threaded Physics: To increase performance, Unity added multi-threaded physics in later versions. It distributes physics calculations over numerous CPU cores, increasing simulation efficiency. To use this functionality, make sure to configure your project in the Project Settings for Physics Jobs and Burst.
13. Third-party Physics Engines: Because Unity is extensible, you can incorporate third-party physics engines if the built-in physics system is insufficient. For more specific applications, some developers prefer complex physics engines such as NVIDIA PhysX, Havok, or Bullet.

CHAPTER VI
[Shader Programming]

Shader programming in Unity is a specialist discipline of game development that entails designing custom shaders to control how your Unity game's graphics and visual effects are generated. Shaders are short programs that run directly on the GPU (Graphics Processing Unit) and are written in a shader language such as ShaderLab (a Unity-specific language) or HLSL (High-Level Shading Language). They govern how each pixel and vertex in a 3D model should be displayed on the screen.

Topics that shader programming includes:

1. Types of Shaders:
   Vertex Shaders: These manipulate the properties of individual vertices in 3D models, such as position, color, and texture coordinates.
   Fragment (Pixel) Shaders: These determine the color of individual pixels on the screen, taking into account lighting, texturing, and other visual effects.
   Geometry Shaders: These are less commonly used but allow you to manipulate the geometry of 3D models in real-time.
2. Shader Languages:
   Unity primarily uses ShaderLab and Cg (C for Graphics) or HLSL for shader programming. ShaderLab is a high-level language that simplifies shader creation, while Cg and HLSL are low-level languages that offer more control but can be more complex.
3. Shader Elements: Shaders are made up of several components such as properties, subshaders, passes, and shader programs. Shader parameters can be exposed to the Unity Editor via properties for easy adjustment.
4. Shader Graph: Shader Graph is a visual tool provided by Unity that allows developers to generate shaders without writing code. It's a node-based interface for artists and designers that facilitates shader production.
5. Shader Effects: Shaders are frequently used to generate visual effects such as realistic lighting (e.g., Phong or PBR shaders), water simulations, cel shading, and others.
6. Shader Inclusion: Shaders can be used in Unity by connecting them to materials and then applying those materials to 3D objects. This procedure determines how each object in the scene is represented.
7. Performance: Good performance requires efficient shader programming. Inefficient shaders can saturate the GPU, resulting in reduced frame rates. Profiling and optimization are critical elements in the creation of shaders.
8. Shader Compilation: Shaders are compiled by Unity for certain platforms and graphics cards. To ensure compatibility, you should test your shaders on a variety of hardware.
9. Built-in Shaders in Unity: Unity includes a number of built-in shaders for typical use cases, such as the Standard Shader for PBR rendering. These can serve as a fantastic beginning point for a variety of projects.

10. Custom Shaders: In order to accomplish certain aesthetic effects or enhance performance in your game, you may need to design custom shaders. Unity gives you the freedom to do so.

Shader programming in Unity can be a powerful tool for creating aesthetically appealing and unique game experiences, but it does necessitate a solid understanding of graphics programming as well as the Unity engine. It's frequently utilized by developers that need to stretch the engine's capabilities or create customized visual effects.

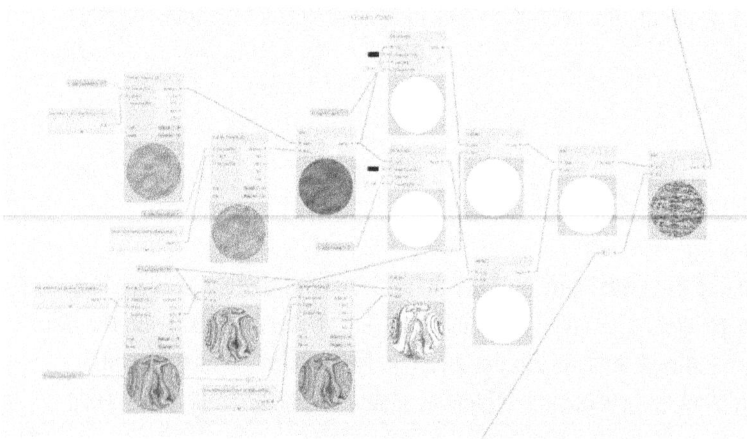

Heat Distortion Effect:

Using shader programming to create a cool project in Unity can be a fun and rewarding experience. In this introduction, I'll lead you through a simple project in which you'll use a shader to produce a "Heat Distortion" effect. This effect creates the illusion that the air above a heated surface is shimmering due to the heat. For someone new to shader programming, it's a visually pleasing and reasonably simple project.
Create a plane in your scene (GameObject > 3D Object > Plane). This will be the "hot surface" that causes the distortion.
Make a Material Right-click in the Assets box and select Make a Material. Give it a name like "HeatDistortionMaterial."
To open the material in the Inspector, double-click it.
Make a Shader Create a new Shader by right-clicking in the Assets window and selecting "Shader" from the Create menu. And name it "HeatDistortionShader".
To open the "HeatDistortionShader" code editor, double-click it.Simply replace the default shader code with a heat distortion shader. Here's a simple example to get you started:

```
Shader "Custom/HeatDistortionShader"

    Properties
    {
        _MainTex ("Texture", 2D) = "white" {}
        _DistortionStrength ("Distortion Strength", Range(0, 1)) = 0.1
        _Speed ("Distortion Speed", Range(0, 10)) = 5
    }

    SubShader
    {
        Tags { "Queue" = "Transparent" }
        Pass
        {
            CGPROGRAM
            #pragma vertex vert
            #pragma fragment frag
            #include "UnityCG.cginc"

            struct appdata_t
            {
                float4 vertex : POSITION;
                float2 texcoord : TEXCOORD0;
            };

            struct v2f
            {
                float2 texcoord : TEXCOORD0;
                float4 vertex : SV_POSITION;
            };

            sampler2D _MainTex;
            float _DistortionStrength;
            float _Speed;

            v2f vert(appdata_t v)
            {
                v2f o;
                o.vertex = UnityObjectToClipPos(v.vertex);
                o.texcoord = v.texcoord;
                return o;
            }

            half4 frag(v2f i) : SV_Target
            {
                float2 uv = i.texcoord;
                uv += float2(sin(uv.y * _Speed), cos(uv.x * _Speed)) * _DistortionStrength;
                return tex2D(_MainTex, uv);
            }
            ENDCG
        }
    }
```

This shader uses a simple UV distortion effect to simulate heat distortion. Return to Unity and choose the"HeatDistortionMaterial" you made before. Change the Shader in the Inspector to "Custom/HeatDistortionShader."
In your scenario, select the plane. Assign the "HeatDistortionMaterial" to the Mesh Renderer component's Material slot in the Inspector. Import a texture (for example, a noise texture) to be used for heat distortion. Place it in the "_MainTex"slot of your "HeatDistortionMaterial". To get the appropriate heat distortion effect, adjust the material's "_DistortionStrength" and "_Speed" attributes.

Play out your scene. You should be able to see the heat distortion effect on the plane, which gives the appearance of heat shimmering.

By developing a visually pleasing heat distortion effect, this project provides a basic introduction to shader programming in Unity. You can expand and customize this project by experimenting with more advanced shader techniques and effects like refraction, reflection, and more intricate animations. Shader programming provides limitless opportunities for generating one-of-a-kind visual experiences in your games and interactive applications.

Portal shader:

```
Shader "Custom/PortalShader"
{
    Properties
    {
        _MainTex ("Texture", 2D) = "white" {}
        _ReflectionTex ("Reflection Texture", 2D) = "white" {}
        _RefractionTex ("Refraction Texture", 2D) = "white" {}
        _ReflectionStrength ("Reflection Strength", Range(0, 1)) = 0.5
        _RefractionStrength ("Refraction Strength", Range(0, 1)) = 0.5
        _Distortion ("Distortion", Range(0, 1)) = 0.1
    }

    SubShader
    {
        Tags { "Queue" = "Transparent" }
        Pass
        {
            CGPROGRAM
            #pragma vertex vert
            #pragma fragment frag
            #include "UnityCG.cginc"

            struct appdata_t
            {
                float4 vertex : POSITION;
                float2 texcoord : TEXCOORD0;
            };

            struct v2f
            {
                float2 texcoord : TEXCOORD0;
                float4 vertex : SV_POSITION;
            };

            sampler2D _MainTex;
            sampler2D _ReflectionTex;
            sampler2D _RefractionTex;
            float _ReflectionStrength;
            float _RefractionStrength;
            float _Distortion;

            v2f vert(appdata_t v)
            {
                v2f o;
                o.vertex = UnityObjectToClipPos(v.vertex);
                o.texcoord = v.texcoord;
                return o;
            }

            half4 frag(v2f i) : SV_Target
            {
                // Implement reflection and refraction effects here
                // You'll need to calculate the reflection and refraction vectors and sample textures accordingly.

                return tex2D(_MainTex, i.texcoord);
            }
            ENDCG
        }
    }
}
```

Making a portal shader is a more difficult undertaking that requires extensive shader computations and camera setup. This project provides an excellent opportunity to experiment with shader programming in Unity and produce an innovative and visually appealing effect in your game or application. You can expand on this project by adding features like recursive portal rendering or portal interactions with game items.

Space Nebula Shader:

A more sophisticated shader programming project is to create a "Space Nebula Shader" in Unity. Space nebulae are gorgeous and complicated cosmic occurrences, and this shader project seeks to recreate their brilliant, swirling colors and patterns, creating a visually appealing impression.

Create a quad (a 2D plane) in your scene. This will serve as the canvas for your space nebula effect.

Implement procedural production of a space nebula in your shader code. To recreate the fine intricacies observed in real nebulae, you will need to develop patterns and colors.

Add advanced elements such as: to make the nebula look more realistic and visually appealing. Swirling patterns: Create the swirling patterns observed in nebulae by using noise algorithms. Color variations: Create the brilliant hues observed in nebulae in space. By scrolling the nebula material over time, you may create a sense of depth and motion.

Define shader properties that will allow you to adjust the nebula's appearance. Color gradients, pattern scaling, speed of motion, and density are examples of these qualities.

Consider using camera effects like depth of field, starfield background, and bloom to enhance the space scene.

Test the nebula shader on your scene. To fine-tune the appearance of the nebula, change the parameters and interact with it.

If you want to take it a step further, add animation to the nebula. This may entail animating the swirling patterns, which would cause the nebula to vary and evolve over time.

Consider using advanced lighting techniques like as subsurface scattering or global illumination to make the nebula interact with the lighting in your scene.
Creating a space nebula shader is a complex undertaking that necessitates a solid foundation in shader programming, mathematics, and procedural content production. It's a fantastic opportunity to experiment with intricate and aesthetically striking effects.

While this project may appear difficult, the aesthetic impact it may have on your game or simulation can be extremely rewarding. To obtain the ideal nebula appearance, expect a large amount of trial and iteration. Additionally, use sophisticated shader programming materials and tutorials to properly complete the many elements of this project.

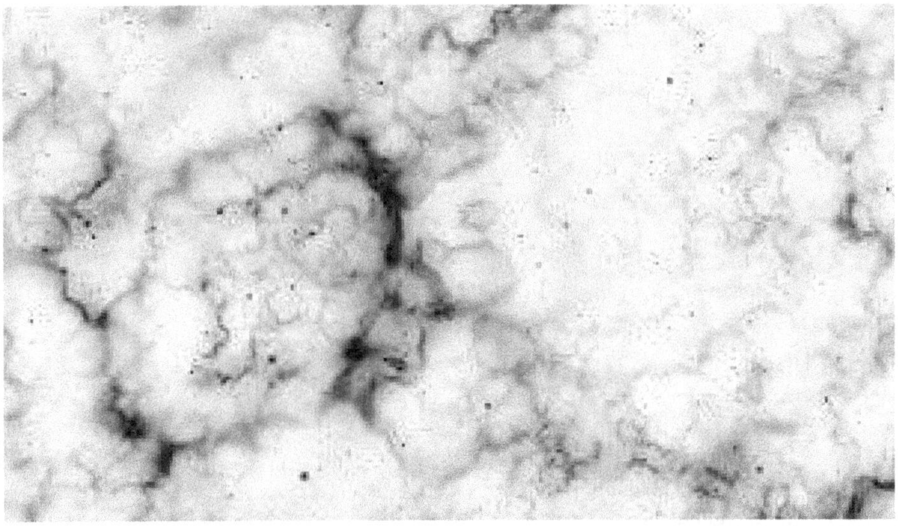

Creating a comprehensive space nebula shader is a difficult process that requires a significant amount of code. I'll supply you with a simple example of a space nebula shader to get you started. This example, however, does not represent the entire complexities of an actual space nebula, but it does highlight some fundamental shader principles. Let's start by making a simple swirling pattern shader with color variations.

```
Shader "Custom/SpaceNebulaShader"
{
    Properties
    {
        _MainTex ("Nebula Texture", 2D) = "white" {}
        _Scale ("Pattern Scale", Range(1, 10)) = 5
        _Speed ("Pattern Speed", Range(0, 2)) = 0.5
    }

    SubShader
    {
        Tags { "Queue" = "Transparent" }
        Pass
        {
            CGPROGRAM
            #pragma vertex vert
            #pragma fragment frag
            #include "UnityCG.cginc"

            struct appdata_t
            {
                float4 vertex : POSITION;
                float2 texcoord : TEXCOORD0;
            };

            struct v2f
            {
                float2 texcoord : TEXCOORD0;
                float4 vertex : SV_POSITION;
            };

            sampler2D _MainTex;
            float _Scale;
            float _Speed;

            v2f vert(appdata_t v)
            {
                v2f o;
                o.vertex = UnityObjectToClipPos(v.vertex);
                o.texcoord = v.texcoord;
                return o;
            }

            half4 frag(v2f i) : SV_Target
            {
                float2 uv = i.texcoord;
                uv += float2(cos(uv.y * _Scale), sin(uv.x * _Scale)) * _Speed;
                half4 nebulaColor = tex2D(_MainTex, uv);
                return nebulaColor;
            }
            ENDCG
        }
    }
}
```

Properties: Three properties are defined in this shader.

_MainTex: The nebula's main texture.
_Scale: A property that allows you to change the scale of the swirling pattern.
_Speed: A property that controls the rotation speed of the pattern.
SubShader and Pass: This is the standard shader structure.

vertex and fragment Functions: The vert function is in charge of altering the mesh's vertices. It simply passes through the position and texture coordinates in this simple example. The fragment shader determines the color of each pixel using the frag function.

uv Coordinates: We sample the texture using uv coordinates. To recreate the whirling appearance, we alter these coordinates by adding a pattern of sin and cos functions. The _Scale and _Speed properties regulate the size and speed of the pattern, respectively.

Texture Sampling: Using the changed uv coordinates, we sample the _MainTex texture. The sampled color is returned as the fragment's final color.

In actuality, building a genuine space nebula shader would require considerably more complex procedural generation, such as more advanced noise algorithms, numerous layers of patterns, and color changes. Furthermore, to produce a realistic appearance, the shader would need to be integrated into a complete scene, animated, and have lighting effects added.

To get a more believable space nebula look, you can improve this shader by trying with more complicated noise functions, merging numerous textures, and experimenting with other techniques. Prepare to spend time trying and iterating in order to obtain the desired outcome.

Here are the basics of coding in shader programming in Unity:

1. Shader Types:
   Vertex Shader: This shader type manipulates the vertices' positions and attributes in 3D models.
   Fragment Shader (Pixel Shader): This shader type affects how 3D objects are represented by determining the color of individual pixels on the screen.
2. Shader Programming Languages:
   ShaderLab is the primary shader development tool used by Unity. It's a high-level language that makes creating shaders easier.
   For low-level shader instructions, ShaderLab is frequently paired with CG (C for Graphics) or HLSL (High-Level Shading Language).
3. Shader Elements:
   Properties: These are settings that are visible in Unity's Material Inspector and allow artists and designers to modify shader functionality.
   Shader code can have several sub shaders to support different hardware levels.
   Passes: Each subshader has one or more passes that specify how the shader interacts with lights, shadows, and other effects.
   Shader programs, which contain vertex and fragment shader parts, are created in ShaderLab.
4. Vertex Shaders: Typically, vertex shaders alter the vertex position in 3D space. They can also send information to fragment shaders such as texture coordinates and illumination information.
5. Fragment Shaders: The final color of each pixel is determined by fragment shaders. They have the ability to sample textures, adjust lighting, and produce visual effects.
6. Shader Characteristics:
   ShaderLab allows you to define properties that expose variables to the Unity Editor. Colors, textures, and numeric values, for example, can all have qualities.
   These parameters improve the usability of shaders by allowing you to change shader behavior without changing the code.
7. Input Structures: In vertex and fragment shaders, data is passed between shader stages using input structures such as appdata_t and v2f. The data received by the vertex shader is defined by appdata_t, but the data provided to the fragment shader is defined by v2f.
8. Texture Sampling: You use sampler2D to represent a 2D texture and the tex2D() method to sample it in shaders. Texture coordinates (often in float2 or half2 format) are used to determine where to sample on the texture.

9. Output Color: The output color is specified in the fragment shader using the half4 data type and returned using return. The fragment shader determines the final pixel color and sends it to the screen.

These fundamentals should give you a solid understanding of shader programming in Unity. It's critical to practice, experiment, and investigate more sophisticated topics while working on shader projects to become proficient. Unity's official documentation and online tutorials might be useful resources for furthering your education.

The Basics of CG:

Understanding the syntax and principles relevant to shader development is required for the basics of Cg (C for Graphics) or Cg/HLSL (High-Level Shading Language) as used in shader programming within Unity. Here's a high-level overview:

1. Data Types:

Scalars: float, half, fixed, int, uint, bool.
Vectors: float2, float3, float4, int2, etc.
Matrices: float2x2, float3x3, float4x4, int2x2, etc.
Sampler Types: sampler2D, samplerCube, etc., for textures.
Structures: You can define custom structures to organize your data.

2. Variables:

Variables store data and include system-defined types and user-defined types within structures. You can declare variables using keywords like float, int, or sampler2D followed by the variable name.
Example: float4 color;

3. Functions:

In Unity shaders, shader code is arranged into functions, which include vertex and fragment functions. Custom functions can be defined to encapsulate logic and increase code reusability.

4. Main Function:

The vertex and fragment methods are the entry points for Unity shaders.
The vertices are transformed by the vertex function, whereas the pixel colors are calculated by the fragment function.

5. Semantics:

Semantics are utilized in the vertex function to indicate the meaning of variables (for example, POSITION for vertex position, TEXCOORD0 for texture coordinates).
Semantics describe which data is automatically interpolated from the vertices in the fragment function.

6. Operators:

Cg supports a wide range of operators, including arithmetic (+, -, *, /), comparison (, >, =, >=, ==,!=), logical (&&, ||,!) and more.

7. Conditional Statements:

Conditional statements (if, else if, else) allow you to make decisions based on conditions.

8. Loops:

Shader code usually avoids loops, as they can be costly. However, Unity's Shader Graph and ShaderLab allow for more structured iteration.

9. Macros:

Macros are defined using #define and used for creating constants or for conditional compilation. Example: #define PI 3.14159.

10. Preprocessor Directives:

#pragma directives are used to specify certain instructions for the compiler, such as which function should be the entry point.

11. Built-in Functions:

Cg/HLSL provides numerous built-in functions for mathematical operations, texturing, and more. Example: tex2D() for texture sampling.

12. Comments:

You can add comments to make code more readable using // for single-line comments and /* */ for multi-line comments.

13. Data Flow:

Data flows from the vertex to the fragment function. Vertex data, including attributes like position and normals, can be transformed and passed to the fragment function for shading.

These are the foundational elements of Cg/HLSL shader programming in Unity. As you go deeper into shader development, you'll explore advanced topics like lighting models, normal mapping, shadowing, and advanced texture techniques. To create complex shaders. Let's get more information to code a better shaders:

14. Variables and Data Types:

Variables might be global, local, or uniform in nature. Global variables are shared by all shader instances, while local variables are exclusive to a function and uniform variables are shared by all shader stages (vertex, fragment, and so on).

15. Texture Sampling:

Texture sampling is an important aspect of shader programming. To sample textures, use the tex2D() function, and you can adjust texture behavior by using various filtering modes and wrap modes.

16. Vectors and Matrices:

Cg/HLSL supports vector and matrix types, which makes it easy to work with 2D and 3D graphics data. A float4 vector, for example, can be used to represent positions in 3D space.

17. Mathematical Functions:

Shader programming frequently incorporates trigonometric functions (sin, cos, tan), exponentials (exp, log), and other operations (abs, sqrt, lerp, and so on).

18. Normal Mapping:

Normal maps are used to enhance the surface detail of 3D models. Normal mapping is the process of modifying the surface normals at each pixel in order to imitate surface bumps and defects.

19. Lighting Models:

Shaders can simulate how light interacts with surfaces by implementing various lighting models such as Lambertian diffuse reflection, Blinn-Phong specular reflection, and others.

20. Texture Coordinates:

Texture coordinates (TEXCOORD0, TEXCOORD1, etc.) allow you to map textures onto 3D models. You can manipulate these coordinates to create various texture effects.

21. Blending and Transparency:

The alpha value (half4) in the fragment shader can be used to manage transparency and blending. This enables the creation of transparent materials as well as complicated compositing effects.

22. Normalization:

Normalizing vectors (through the normalize() function) is critical for ensuring proper lighting calculations.

23. Shadow Mapping:

Shadow mapping is a technique for simulating the shadows cast by three-dimensional objects in a scene. Shaders can use shadow mapping to create realistic shadow effects.

24. Specular Reflection:

When exposed to light, specular reflection is the highlight that emerges on shiny surfaces. To produce realistic materials, shaders can use specular reflection calculations.

25. GPU Optimization:

It is critical to optimize shaders for GPU performance. Rendering time can be considerably improved by using techniques such as batching, LOD (Level of Detail), and reducing texture fetches.

This advanced material should help you grasp shader programming in Unity better. To design complicated and aesthetically attractive shaders for your games and simulations, you must combine these notions with actual implementation and experimentation. Remember that shader programming is both an art and a science, and that achieving the desired visual effects typically necessitates iteration and fine-tuning.

CHAPTER VII
[AI]

Integrating AI into Unity, a popular game creation engine, brings up a world of possibilities for developing immersive and dynamic gameplay experiences. AI in Unity allows developers to create intelligent, lifelike non-player characters (NPCs), responsive opponents, and dynamic virtual surroundings. In this introduction, we will look at the essential principles and tools that enable AI programming in Unity.

1. AI in Unity: AI in Unity is the application of methods and techniques that allow game characters and objects to show intelligent behaviors, respond to user input, and make decisions depending on their surroundings. These AI systems are critical for developing difficult opponents, realistic simulations, and increasing user interest.

2. AI Tools and Components: Unity provides a variety of AI tools and components, including:

NavMesh: Unity's NavMesh technology allows you to construct navigation meshes for your characters, which allows them to be aware of their surroundings, navigate their way about, and avoid obstacles.

Pathfinding using the A* Algorithm:* The A* algorithm is often used for pathfinding, allowing characters to discover the shortest path from one location to another while avoiding obstacles.

Behavior trees are visual scripting tools that are used to develop and manage AI behaviors in a modular and intuitive manner.

AI Agents: Agents in Unity's AI system can be used to control NPCs and other objects with specified behaviors such as following waypoints or pursuing the player.

3. C# scripting: C# is extensively used by Unity for scripting AI behaviors. Custom scripts can be written by developers to govern AI behaviors and judgments. These scripts can be applied to game objects to control how they behave and react in various situations.

4. Machine Learning and Reinforcement Learning: Unity has machine learning and reinforcement learning tools, allowing AI agents to be trained using external libraries such as TensorFlow or Unity's ML-Agents toolkit. This is especially useful for developing adaptable and learning AI.

5. AI Applications: AI is used in a variety of game genres, including RPGs, shooters, strategy games, and simulations. It can be used to control characters, make decisions, control enemies, and even generate procedural material.
6. Challenges: Using AI in Unity can be difficult, especially when dealing with complicated behaviors and optimization. Balancing realism and performance is critical, as poorly tuned AI can have a severe influence on game performance.

To summarize, AI in Unity is an important part of modern game creation since it allows creators to create dynamic and compelling gameplay experiences. Understanding and mastering AI ideas in Unity may help you breathe life into your virtual worlds, whether you're making a simple puzzle game or a complex open-world adventure. You can bring intelligent and responsive AI characters and systems to your games with the correct tools, knowledge, and creativity.

Let's dive a bit deeper into advanced AI concepts and techniques in Unity:

1. Machine Learning and Reinforcement Learning: Integrating machine learning and reinforcement learning is a common feature of advanced AI in Unity. The ML-Agents toolkit in Unity allows you to train AI agents to learn and adapt to various environments. Custom machine learning methods for complicated AI behaviors can be implemented using external libraries such as TensorFlow. This is especially beneficial for developing artificial intelligence that can learn from player interactions, adapt to changing game conditions, and even optimize their strategy over time.

2. Neural Networks: Deep learning, a subset of machine learning, is important in advanced AI development. Unity includes support for neural networks, which may be used to create sophisticated AI models for tasks like character animation, natural language processing, and picture recognition. The Barracuda inference engine in Unity allows you to efficiently run trained neural networks within your game.

3. Procedural Content Generation: Advanced artificial intelligence can be used to generate game content on the fly. You can utilize AI algorithms, for example, to build procedurally generated levels, sceneries, or objects, ensuring that no two playthroughs are the identical. This gives your games more depth and replayability.

4. Natural Language Processing (NLP): Using NLP in Unity, you can interact with AI characters via voice or text. This has the potential to improve storyline and player engagement. You can add chatbots, NPCs with conversational abilities, or text-based gaming interfaces using third-party NLP frameworks and APIs.

5. Multi-Agent Systems: In complex games or simulations, AI systems with several interacting agents may be required. Unity offers tools and strategies for coordinating the behavior of several AI entities, such as simulating city traffic, directing large-scale combat, and generating social simulations with multiple people.

6. Advanced Pathfinding and Crowd Simulation: The NavMesh system in Unity may be enhanced to handle more complex pathfinding scenarios. This features adaptive pathfinding for shifting situations, crowd simulation for dealing with huge groups of characters, and AI algorithms for optimal crowd management.

7. Behavior Trees and Finite State Machines (FSM): While behavior trees and FSMs are not novel concepts, powerful AI can develop complicated behavior trees and FSMs that manage difficult decision-making processes. Subtrees, decorators, and parallel jobs can be used to generate highly adaptive and sophisticated AI behaviors.

8. VR/AR and Spatial Understanding: AI can be utilized to understand the spatial context in virtual and augmented reality applications produced in Unity. AI can aid in object recognition, tracking, and providing more immersive interactions in VR and AR experiences.

9. Autonomous Vehicles and Simulations: AI systems for simulating autonomous cars and robotics can be created using Unity. You may create superior artificial intelligence for self-driving cars, drones, and robots and test and train them in simulated situations before deploying them in the real world.

10. Optimization and Performance: Advanced AI systems frequently require rigorous optimization to enable smooth operation within the game. Advanced profiling, parallel processing, and using Unity's Job System and Burst Compiler for improved performance are all possibilities.

In summary, advanced AI in Unity grows into a variety of complicated domains such as machine learning, procedural content generation, natural language processing (NLP), multi-agent systems, and extremely detailed pathfinding. These advanced AI concepts have the potential to transform your game or simulation into a highly engaging and intelligent experience, but they frequently necessitate a thorough understanding of AI algorithms, optimization techniques, and Unity's broad toolkit to effectively apply.

How to make an advanced AI project:

Developing a sophisticated AI project in Unity requires many parts and can be a difficult task. Let's sketch out a high-level plan for a project that integrates a variety of advanced AI approaches and concepts. We'll develop an example project involving a simulated city with autonomous vehicles that navigate using machine learning.

Simulation of Autonomous Vehicles in a Virtual City:

1. Project Configuration:
Begin by making a new Unity project. Import any assets and packages that are required, including the Unity ML-Agents toolkit for machine learning integration.

2. Design of the Environment:
Using Unity's landscape and construction tools, create a virtual city setting. Create realistic 3D models of automobiles, pedestrians, and traffic signals to populate the city. Make a road network, with lanes and traffic restrictions.

3. Autonomous Vehicle Agents:

Create autonomous vehicle agents with 3D models and rigidbody components. Set up the agents' behavior and learning algorithms with ML-Agents. Define agent goals, such as achieving locations, following traffic regulations, and avoiding collisions.

4. Integration of Machine Learning:

Using the ML-Agents toolbox, set up the machine learning environment. Define the agents' observation and action spaces. Consider inputs such as position, speed, and proximity to other vehicles and traffic signals when making observations. To influence agent behavior and offer feedback, use reward functions. Reinforcement learning algorithms are used to train the agents. To train agents, you can utilize Unity's ML-Agents or external machine learning frameworks such as TensorFlow.

5. Simulation of Traffic:

Realistic traffic simulation, including traffic lights and pedestrian crossings, should be implemented.Scripts should be written to handle traffic flow and signal changes. These traffic aspects should be detectable and respondable by agents.

6. Neural Network Models:

Create neural network models to aid the decision-making process of the agents. Train models to navigate city environments while following traffic laws and avoiding crashes.

7. Generation of Procedural Content:

Create dynamic traffic circumstances and difficulties by incorporating a procedural content creation engine.
Consider employing algorithms to create various vehicle kinds, road layouts, and pedestrian behavior patterns.
8. Interaction with Users:

Create a user interface for interacting with the simulation. This may include the ability to alter traffic conditions, control individual vehicles, and track training progress.

9. Evaluation and testing:

Evaluate the performance of the trained agents in various settings. To evaluate the agents' behavior, use measures such as traffic flow efficiency, safety, and adherence to traffic rules.

10. Performance and Optimization:

Because conducting machine learning simulations might be resource-intensive, optimize the project for performance. Consider using Unity's Job System and Burst Compiler to boost performance.

11. Visualization and Testing:

Use visualization tools to examine and comprehend the AI agents' decision-making processes and neural network outputs. Make debugging tools to track agent behavior during training and testing.

Machine learning, procedural content production, intricate traffic simulation, and interaction with the Unity environment are all part of this advanced AI project. Remember that establishing such a project can be time-consuming and difficult, so be prepared to put in a lot of effort into its creation and testing. Furthermore, keeping up with the newest breakthroughs in AI and Unity is critical for success in this quest.

Let's start with the project setup. This is a crucial step to ensure that you have the right environment and tools in place for developing your advanced AI project in Unity.

Project setup:

1.Launch a New Unity Project:

Open Unity and choose "New" to start a new project.

Decide on a project name and location.

Choose the correct Unity version for your project.

2.Import Necessary Assets:

Consider using Unity's Asset Store or other 3D modeling program to buy city-related assets such as buildings, vehicles, and pedestrians to create a virtual city scene.
If you intend to apply reinforcement learning for your autonomous vehicles, import the Unity ML-Agents Toolkit. It's available on the Unity GitHub repository.

3.Setup of the Scene:

Make a fresh scene for your project.
Add topography, roads, buildings, and other materials to your virtual city setting.

4.Rigidbody and Collider Components:

Create 3D models of your autonomous vehicle agents and apply Rigidbody components to them.
To enable accurate collision detection, connect Collider components.

5.Camera Configuration:

Set up a camera or cameras to observe and record the simulation.
Set camera angles and placements to watch the agents' actions.

6.Machine Learning Environment:

Set up the ML-Agents environment if you're using Unity's ML-Agents:
Define your agents' observation and action spaces. These environments define what the agents can see and how they can interact with their surroundings.
Create reward functions that provide feedback to agents while they are training.
Set up the environment so that it can run in either training or inference mode.

7.Prefab Agents:

Create agent prefabs that include the agent's 3D model, scripts, and any other components that are required.
Define the agent's starting positions, aims, and basic city circumstances.

8.Training Environment:

Set up the training environment if you intend to teach your autonomous vehicles:
Configure the training configuration files for Unity ML-Agents.
Create a training pipeline that will manage the training process, including the integration of TensorFlow or other machine learning libraries.

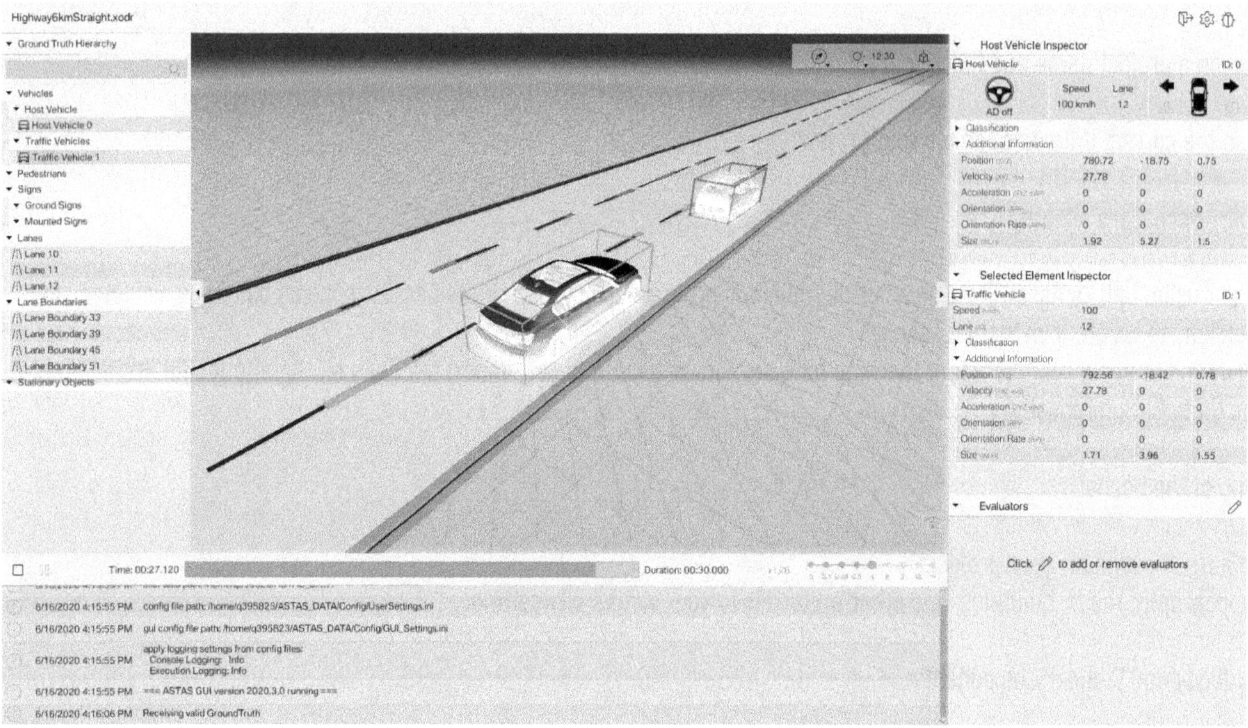

9.User Interface:

If you want to interact with the simulation or monitor training, utilize Unity's UI system to create and build a user interface.

10.Version Control:

Consider using version control tools such as Git to track changes in your project and efficiently work with others.

After you've finished setting up your project, you can begin developing the virtual city environment and autonomous vehicle agents. The configuration serves as the foundation for building and testing your sophisticated AI project in Unity.

Environment Design:

Let's go on to developing the virtual city setting in Unity for your advanced AI project. This is a critical step in establishing a realistic and immersive environment for your autonomous car simulation.

City Layout and Terrain:

Begin by creating a layout for your virtual city. Plan the road system, intersections, and locations in which your agents will operate.
Create the city's landscape, including roads, walkways, parks, and other features, using Unity's terrain system.
Create the desired topography and urban features by sculpting the terrain.

Structures and buildings:

Build 3D models of buildings, houses, offices, and other structures to populate your city. These models can be created or imported.
Make sure the structures are properly scaled and placed in the scene.

Road System:

Make a road network that connects various parts of the city. To imitate real-world traffic situations, define lanes, intersections, and road signs. Place road markings and signage to direct traffic.

Elements of the Traffic:

Increase the number of traffic signals at intersections. To regulate traffic flow, you may need to script their behavior.
For realistic pedestrian interactions, including pedestrian crossings and sidewalks.
To represent automobiles and pedestrians, use 3D models or Unity's basic assets.

Elements from Nature:

Integrate natural elements such as trees, parks, and bodies of water to improve the visual appeal of the city.
To add grass, dirt, and other natural textures, use Unity's terrain painting tools.

Weather and lighting:

Use dynamic lighting and environmental effects to replicate day and night cycles, as well as various weather situations.
To achieve realistic lighting and shadows, use Unity's lighting and rendering features.
Interiors (Optional):

Design the interiors of buildings, workplaces, or other accessible areas if your project incorporates interiors. This may necessitate more 3D modeling and coding.

Customization and Details:

Take note to the smaller things, such as road signs, street lamps, benches, and other urban aspects.
Customize the city's appearance to meet the topic and goals of your project.

Optimization:

Optimize the scene for performance on a regular basis. To ensure seamless gameplay, use techniques such as occlusion culling and LOD (Level of Detail).

Colliders and Mesh Navigation:

Colliders can be added to buildings, vehicles, and other objects to allow for realistic collision detection.
Create a NavMesh for the city to aid AI agents in pathfinding and navigation.

Sound Design (Optional):

Consider adding ambient sounds and environmental audio to enhance the immersive experience.

Iteration and testing:

Test the city environment with your agents on a regular basis to detect flaws, fine-tune specifics, and verify it fulfills the objectives of your project.

Remember that creating a realistic virtual city can take some time. Take your time to design an aesthetically appealing and practical space. Because your autonomous vehicle agents will rely on this environment for navigation, it must be well-designed and appropriately configured. After building the environment, you can create and deploy the city's autonomous car agents.

Let's create a simple C# script for an autonomous vehicle agent that moves along a predefined path using Unity's NavMesh system Just to understand how the project could be developed. This script assumes you have already set up a NavMesh in your virtual city.

```
using UnityEngine.AI;

public class AutonomousVehicle : MonoBehaviour
{
    private NavMeshAgent navAgent;
    public Transform[] waypoints; // Define an array of waypoints for the vehicle to follow
    private int currentWaypointIndex = 0;

    private void Start()
    {
        navAgent = GetComponent<NavMeshAgent>();
        if (waypoints.Length > 0)
        {
            SetDestinationToWaypoint(0);
        }
    }

    private void Update()
    {
        // Check if the vehicle has reached its current waypoint
        if (navAgent.remainingDistance < 0.1f)
        {
            // Move to the next waypoint
            currentWaypointIndex = (currentWaypointIndex + 1) % waypoints.Length;
            SetDestinationToWaypoint(currentWaypointIndex);
        }
    }

    private void SetDestinationToWaypoint(int index)
    {
        if (index < waypoints.Length)
        {
            navAgent.SetDestination(waypoints[index].position);
        }
    }
```

Here's how to put this script to use:

In the Unity Editor, add this script to your autonomous car GameObject.

Make an empty GameObject for each waypoint in your city. In the Inspector, add these waypoint GameObjects to the script's waypoints array.

Assemble a NavMesh in your scene so the vehicle can navigate the city.

The script will sequentially move the vehicle from one waypoint to another. When it hits a waypoint, it will proceed to the next one automatically.

This is a simple example of autonomous vehicle movement to get you started. Depending on the complexity of your project, you can extend this script to include features such as traffic rule adherence, collision avoidance, and more advanced agent behaviors.

Let's make Autonomous Vehicle Agents in Unity for your advanced AI project. We'll assume you've already set up the virtual city environment, as explained previously. The steps below will walk you through the process of building and configuring the autonomous vehicle agents in your project:

Make an Agent Prefab:

Begin by creating a 3D model of the autonomous vehicle agent. You have the option of creating your own model or importing one.
To enable physics interactions, attach a Rigidbody component to the vehicle.
Include a Collider component, such as a Capsule Collider, to detect collisions.

Script for an Agent:

Create a C# script to govern the agent's behavior. This script should specify how the agent interacts with its surroundings. The agent script may include logic for following waypoints, observing traffic regulations, avoiding obstacles, and making judgments based on sensory inputs, depending on the complexity of your project.

Sensory Information:

Determine the sensory inputs required by the agent to perceive its surroundings. This may include:
Raycasts can be used to identify obstructions and traffic signs.
Sensors that measure the distance between two objects.
Data on the agent's speed, position, and orientation.

Actions:

Define the actions that the agent can perform. This could involve accelerating, braking, and steering in a simple arrangement.
More advanced agents may be required to perform a greater range of behaviors, such as signaling turns, switching lanes, and dealing with complex traffic scenarios.

Machine Learning:

Integrate Unity's ML-Agents Toolkit or an external machine learning framework like TensorFlow if you intend to employ machine learning for agent behavior.
Reinforcement learning or supervised learning approaches can be used to train the agent.

Navigation by Waypoints:

Implement waypoint navigation logic if your agents need to navigate preset paths in the city. For vehicle movement, you can apply the same reasoning as in the previous example script.

Adherence to Traffic Regulations (Optional):

Implement logic to guarantee agents observe laws such as stopping at red lights, ceding to pedestrians, and adhering to speed restrictions if your project requires imitating traffic rules.

Avoiding Obstacles (Optional):

Create obstacle avoidance logic to avoid collisions with other vehicles, pedestrians, and city items.

Interaction with the user (optional):

Create user controls to interact with the agent manually for testing and debugging.
Allow users to modify the agent's behavior or watch its decision-making process.

AI Decision-Making:

Depending on the complexity of your project, use behavior trees, finite state machines, or machine learning models to create AI decision-making.

Performance Enhancement:

Optimize the agent's code and interactions with the environment on a regular basis to maintain smooth gaming and realistic behavior.

Following these steps will lay the groundwork for your autonomous car agents. Depending on the exact requirements and complexity of your project, you may need to expand and personalize the agent's behavior and interaction with the virtual city.

It is critical to create sensory information for your autonomous car agents so that they can perceive and interact with their surroundings. Sensory inputs can include information such as the agent's speed, distance to objects, and traffic lights. In this section, we'll build a simple example of how to implement sensory information in Unity using raycasting.

1. Make empty GameObjects to serve as Sensors:

Create empty GameObjects in your Unity scene to represent sensors on your autonomous vehicle. These can be placed in various locations on the vehicle to simulate sensors (for example, front, sides, and rear).

2. Sensor Script Attachment:

Make a new C# script for each of your sensors. This script will use raycasting to detect obstacles, traffic lights, and other pertinent data.
This script should be attached to each sensor GameObject.

```
using UnityEngine;

public class Sensor : MonoBehaviour
{
    public float maxDetectionDistance = 10.0f;
    public LayerMask detectionLayer; // Set this layer mask to determine what the sensor should detect.

    public bool DetectObstacle()
    {
        RaycastHit hit;
        if (Physics.Raycast(transform.position, transform.forward, out hit, maxDetectionDistance, detectionLayer))
        {
            // An obstacle is detected. You can implement actions or decisions here.
            Debug.DrawRay(transform.position, transform.forward * hit.distance, Color.red);
            return true;
        }
        else
        {
            // No obstacle is detected.
            Debug.DrawRay(transform.position, transform.forward * maxDetectionDistance, Color.green);
            return false;
        }
    }
}
```

3. Set Sensor Parameters:

Set the maxDetectionDistance and detectionLayer values for each sensor GameObject in the Inspector based on your project's needs.
The detectionLayer should be set to include the layers that represent the items that the sensor should detect (for example, obstacles and traffic signals).

4. Integration of Vehicle Agents:
You can access the sensor components and use their information in your autonomous car agent script.

```
public class AutonomousVehicleAgent : MonoBehaviour
{
    // ...

    public Sensor frontSensor; // Attach the front sensor GameObject to this variable in the Inspector.

    // ...

    private void Update()
    {
        // Check the front sensor for obstacles.
        if (frontSensor.DetectObstacle())
        {
            // Implement actions or decisions when an obstacle is detected.
        }

        // ...
    }

    // ...
}
```

This basic example provides a framework for implementing sensors capable of detecting impediments in the route of the vehicle. Depending on the intricacy of your project, you can add more sensors, tweak their behavior, and integrate sensory data into your agent's decision-making processes. Furthermore, advanced projects may employ machine learning techniques for sensing and decision-making, resulting in more sophisticated behavior.

You must specify the behaviors and controls that your autonomous vehicle agent will use to interact with its surroundings before you can develop actions for it. Acceleration, braking, turning, and other motions are examples of actions. In this section, we will write a simple script to control these actions.

Create the Action Script:

Create a C# script for your vehicle agent's actions, which will allow you to control acceleration, braking, and steering.

```
using UnityEngine;

public class VehicleActions : MonoBehaviour
{
    public float accelerationForce = 1000f; // Adjust the values according to your project.
    public float brakingForce = 500f;
    public float maxSpeed = 10f;
    public float steeringSpeed = 5f;

    private Rigidbody rb;

    private void Start()
    {
        rb = GetComponent<Rigidbody>();
    }

    public void Accelerate()
    {
        if (rb.velocity.magnitude < maxSpeed)
        {
            rb.AddForce(transform.forward * accelerationForce);
        }
    }

    public void Brake()
    {
        rb.AddForce(-rb.velocity.normalized * brakingForce);
    }

    public void Steer(float steerInput)
    {
        transform.Rotate(Vector3.up * steerInput * steeringSpeed);
    }
}
```

Attach the Action Script:

Attach the VehicleActions script to your autonomous vehicle agent's GameObject in the Unity Inspector.

Vehicle Agent Integration:

In your vehicle agent script, create a reference to the VehicleActions component and use it to control the agent's actions.

```
public class AutonomousVehicleAgent : MonoBehaviour
{
    public VehicleActions vehicleActions; // Attach the VehicleActions component to this variable in the Inspector.

    // ...

    private void Update()
    {
        // Implement your logic to decide when to accelerate, brake, or steer.
        // For example, you can use the sensor data from the previous step to make decisions.

        if (/* Condition to accelerate */)
        {
            vehicleActions.Accelerate();
        }

        if (/* Condition to brake */)
        {
            vehicleActions.Brake();
        }

        float steerInput = /* Calculate steer input based on your decision logic */;
        vehicleActions.Steer(steerInput);

        // ...
    }

    // ...
}
```

This fundamental example serves as a foundation for performing vehicle operations such as acceleration, braking, and steering. Depending on the complexity of your project, you can add more advanced actions, behaviors, and decision-making logic. More sophisticated AI approaches, like as machine learning, can be used to make the vehicle's actions more adaptive and realistic.

Using Unity to implement machine learning for your autonomous vehicle agents is a difficult task. It necessitates the integration of external machine learning frameworks, the creation of training settings, the design of reward functions, and other tasks. In this post, I'll show you how to get started with machine learning in Unity using the ML-Agents toolbox.

1. Download and install the Unity ML-Agents:

Install the Unity ML-Agents toolkit if you haven't previously done so by following the official installation procedure on the Unity GitHub repository: Unity ML-Agents.

2. Establish a Training Environment:

Create a training environment for your self-driving vehicle agents. This environment should be the same or similar to the one in which the agents will be deployed. Make sure it has the city plan, waypoints, sensors, and any other required components.

3. Establish the Observation and Action Spaces:

Specify the observation space and action space for your agents in the ML-Agents configuration file. The observation space specifies what the agents may see, while the action space specifies the actions they can perform. This is where your sensors and actions are linked to the ML-Agents framework.

4. Create Reward Functions:

Create reward functions to deliver feedback to agents while they are training. These reward functions should encourage desired behaviors while discouraging undesirable ones. You can, for example, offer incentives for staying on the road, observing traffic rules, and avoiding collisions.

5. Establish a Training Academy:

Create a training academy in your Unity project to establish the parameters for your training session, such as the number of agents and training situations.

6.Create Learning Algorithms:

To train your agents, select a reinforcement learning algorithm. Proximal Policy Optimization (PPO), Soft Actor-Critic (SAC), and other methods are supported by ML-Agents. Choose the one that best meets the needs of your project.

7. Establish Training:

Run the ML-Agents training procedure on your Unity project to configure the training process. This process will be repeated through training experiences, with agents learning from their interactions with the environment.

8. Gather Training Data:

Allow the agents to explore the training environment in order to obtain training data. The agents will learn to improve their actions depending on the incentives and observations throughout this phase.

9. Agent Training:

Run the training process, which will include many training episode iterations. Monitor the agents' performance and make necessary hyperparameter adjustments.

10. Save Trained Models:

Once the agents have demonstrated acceptable performance, save their trained models. In your deployment environment, these models can then be employed for inference.

11. Deploy the Trained Agents:

Integrate the trained models into your Unity project to be deployed. This enables the agents to function autonomously in the simulation or game.

12. Evaluation and Fine-Tuning:

Evaluate the agents' performance on a regular basis and, if necessary, fine-tune the trained models and reward functions to achieve the desired behavior.

keep in mind that developing machine learning for autonomous vehicles in Unity is a complicated and iterative process. It frequently necessitates a thorough knowledge of reinforcement learning, neural networks, and the ML-Agents architecture. To attain the desired results, you may need to investigate sophisticated strategies such as curriculum learning and reward structuring. The official ML-Agents literature and tutorials are excellent tools for guiding you through this procedure.

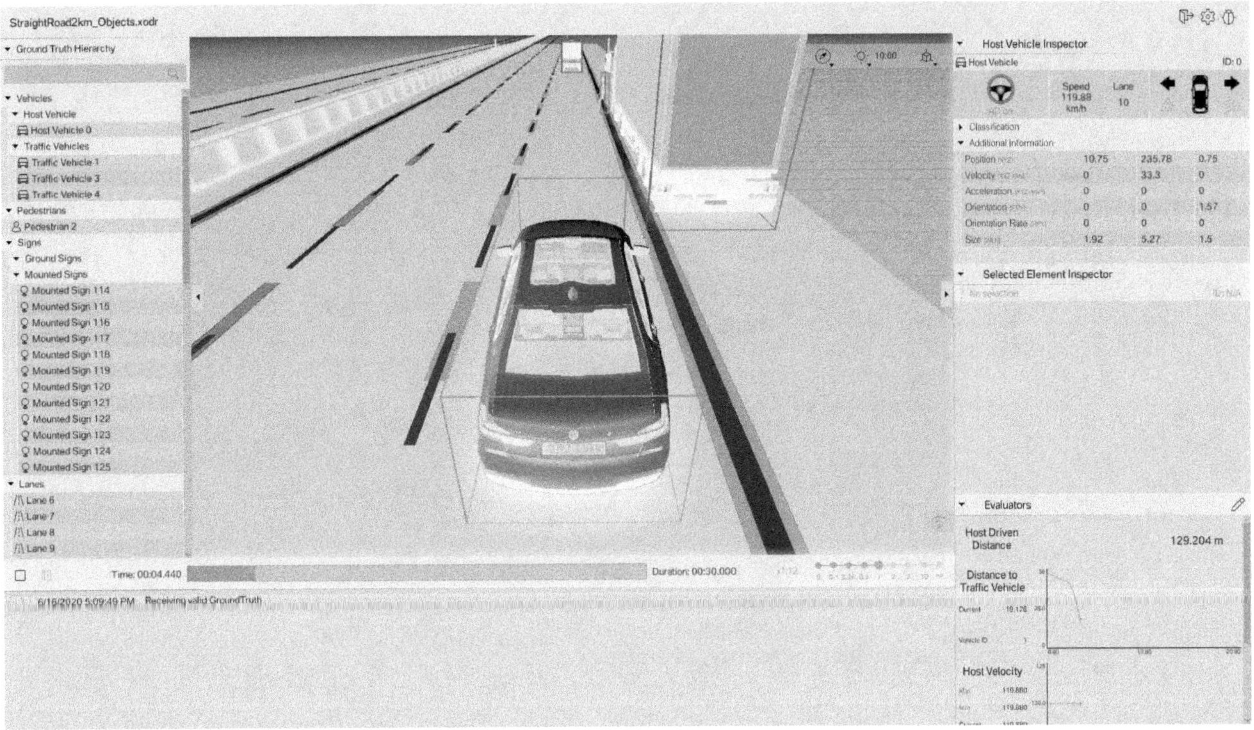

Navigating your autonomous vehicle agents with waypoints is a critical component of directing their movement in the virtual city environment. We'll build a waypoint-based navigation system for your agents in this guide.

1. Establish Waypoints:

Create empty GameObjects in your Unity environment to represent waypoints along the path you want your autonomous car agents to take. These waypoints will determine your agents' route.

2. Waypoint System with Agent Script:

Create a C# script to control the navigation of your autonomous car agents. Here's an example of a waypoint-based script:

```csharp
using UnityEngine;
using UnityEngine.AI;

public class AutonomousVehicleAgent : MonoBehaviour
{
    private NavMeshAgent navAgent;
    public Transform[] waypoints; // Assign waypoints in the Inspector
    private int currentWaypointIndex = 0;

    private void Start()
    {
        navAgent = GetComponent<NavMeshAgent>();
        if (waypoints.Length > 0)
        {
            SetDestinationToWaypoint(0);
        }
    }

    private void Update()
    {
        if (navAgent.remainingDistance < 0.1f)
        {
            currentWaypointIndex = (currentWaypointIndex + 1) % waypoints.Length;
            SetDestinationToWaypoint(currentWaypointIndex);
        }
    }

    private void SetDestinationToWaypoint(int index)
    {
        if (index < waypoints.Length)
        {
            navAgent.SetDestination(waypoints[index].position);
        }
    }
}
```

3. Associate Waypoints with the Agent:

In the Unity Inspector, add the waypoints to the agent script's waypoints array. This controls the order in which waypoints are visited.

4. NavMesh Configuration:

Make sure your scene has a correctly baked NavMesh, which the NavMeshAgent uses for navigation. For more complicated pathfinding scenarios, configure NavMesh layers and areas as needed.

5. Navigation Test:

Run your scene to put your agents' waypoint-based navigation to the test. They should automatically adhere to the waypoints you've set.

6. Logic of Waypoints:

Depending on the intricacy of your project, you can add waypoint-specific logic to your script. You can, for example, force agents to obey traffic regulations, adhere to speed restrictions, or modify their behavior at specific waypoints.

7. Advanced Navigation:

External pathfinding methods, dynamic path changes based on traffic, and complicated traffic rule adherence behaviors can be used for more advanced navigation.
This simplistic example lays the groundwork for your autonomous vehicle agents to use waypoint-based navigation. You can extend this to include more advanced navigation and decision-making, such as traffic regulation adherence, obstacle avoidance, and interactions with other elements in your virtual city, depending on the complexity and requirements of your project.

Traffic standards must be followed in order to create genuine autonomous car behavior in your Unity project. This post will go through how to establish traffic regulation adherence for your autonomous car agents.

1. Establish Traffic Regulations:

Determine the traffic restrictions you want your autonomous car agents to follow. This can involve following traffic laws, stopping at stop signs, surrendering to pedestrians, and adhering to speed restrictions.

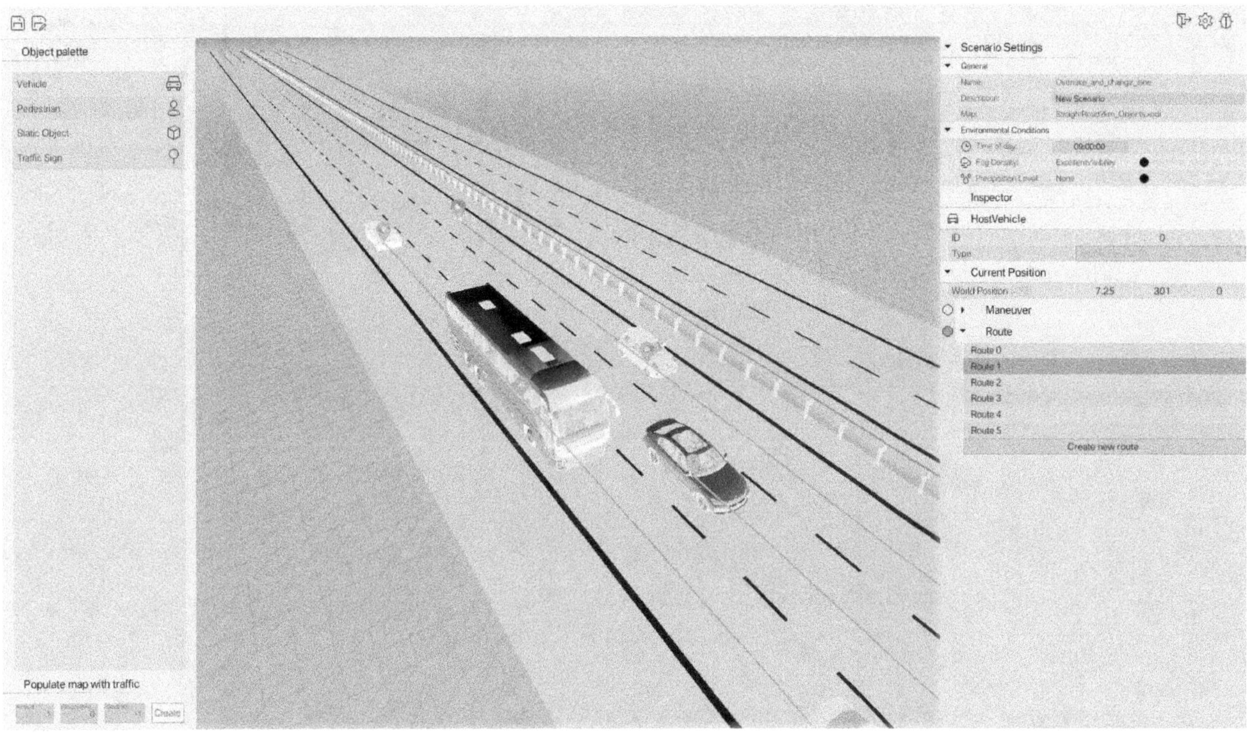

2. Traffic Light Control System:

In your virtual city, create a traffic light system. This includes intersection traffic lights and pedestrian crossings. To represent traffic signals, you can utilize 3D models or Unity UI elements.

3. Agent Script Improvement:

Add logic to the agent script to identify and respond to traffic regulations. Here's an easy way to implement traffic light adherence:

```
using UnityEngine;
using UnityEngine.AI;

public class AutonomousVehicleAgent : MonoBehaviour
{
    private NavMeshAgent navAgent;
    public Transform[] waypoints; // Assign waypoints in the Inspector
    private int currentWaypointIndex = 0;

    public Transform trafficLight; // Attach the traffic light GameObject in the Inspector.
    private TrafficLightController trafficLightController;

    private void Start()
    {
        navAgent = GetComponent < NavMeshAgent();
        trafficLightController = trafficLight.GetComponent<TrafficLightController>();

        if (waypoints.Length > 0)
        {
            SetDestinationToWaypoint(0);
        }
    }

    private void Update()
    {
        if (navAgent.remainingDistance < 0.1f)
        {
            currentWaypointIndex = (currentWaypointIndex + 1) % waypoints.Length;
            SetDestinationToWaypoint(currentWaypointIndex);
        }

        // Check traffic light and adhere to its state
        if (trafficLightController.IsRed())
        {
            navAgent.isStopped = true; // Stop at the red light.
        }
        else
        {
            navAgent.isStopped = false; // Continue when the light is green.
        }
    }

    private void SetDestinationToWaypoint(int index)
    {
        if (index < waypoints.Length)
        {
            navAgent.SetDestination(waypoints[index].position);
        }
    }
}
```

4. Traffic Light Controller.

Create a script, such as TrafficLightController, to control the behavior of traffic lights. The controller should have methods to check the state of the traffic light (red, green, or yellow).

```
using UnityEngine;

public class TrafficLightController : MonoBehaviour
{
    public bool IsRed()
    {
        // Implement logic to check if the traffic light is red.
        // You can use a timer or other mechanisms to control the state of the light.
        return /* true or false based on the state of the traffic light */;
    }
}
```

5. Check for Traffic Light Adherence:

Run your scene to see how well your agents follow traffic light restrictions. Make sure they stop at red lights and continue when the light turns green.

6.Advanced Traffic Regulations:

Additional logic for handling stop signs, pedestrian crossings, speed limits, and interactions with other vehicles and people can be implemented for more advanced traffic law adherence.

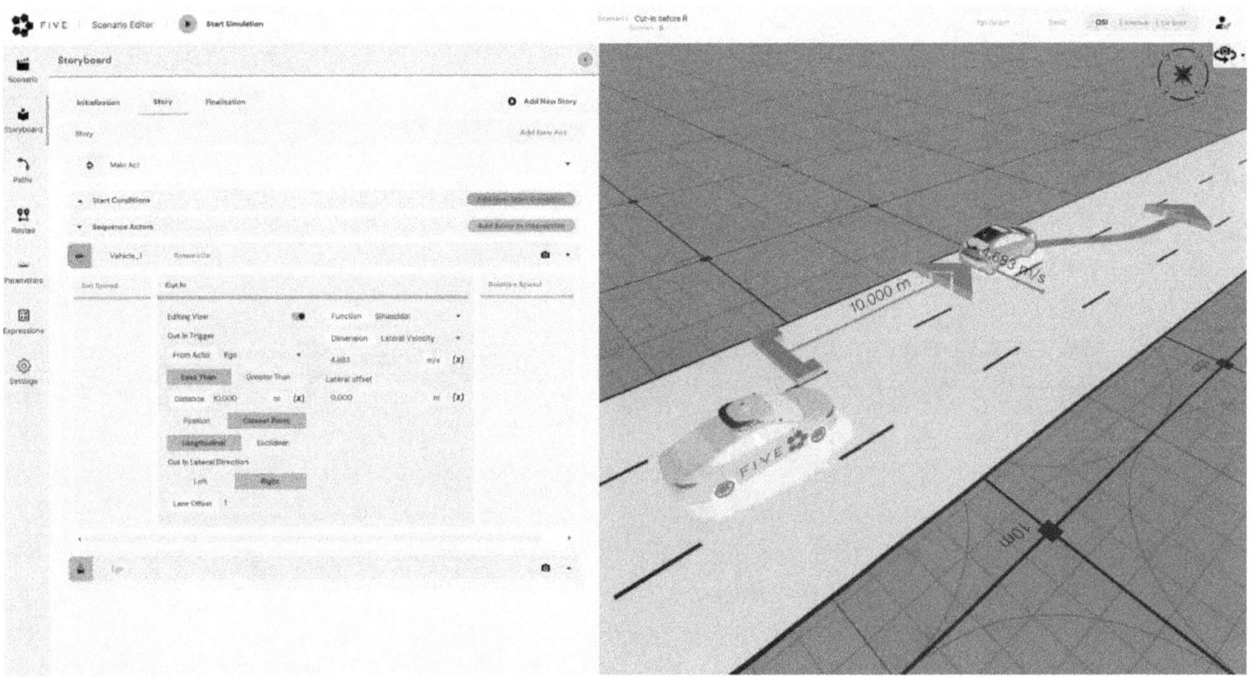

Your autonomous car agents will behave more realistically in your virtual city setting if you enforce traffic regulations. Depending on the complexity of your project, you can incorporate more advanced behaviors and decision-making to ensure correct adherence to traffic standards.

Obstacle avoidance is a critical component for autonomous vehicles to operate through complex settings safely. You can avoid obstacles in Unity by using raycasting and altering your vehicle's path or speed based on detected impediments. Here's how to add obstacle avoidance to your autonomous vehicle agents step by step:

1. Design Obstacle Objects:

Place impediment items (such as other vehicles, pedestrians, or static objects) in your Unity scenario that your autonomous vehicles should avoid. Make certain that these objects have colliders to detect collisions.

2. Agent Script Improvement:

Include obstacle detection and avoidance logic in your agent script. Here's a simplistic example of how to use raycasting to avoid obstacles:

```
using UnityEngine;
using UnityEngine.AI;

public class AutonomousVehicleAgent : MonoBehaviour
{
    private NavMeshAgent navAgent;
    public Transform[] waypoints; // Assign waypoints in the Inspector
    private int currentWaypointIndex = 0;

    public LayerMask obstacleLayer; // Set this layer mask to detect obstacles

    private void Start()
    {
        navAgent = GetComponent<NavMeshAgent>();
        if (waypoints.Length > 0)
        {
            SetDestinationToWaypoint(0);
        }
    }

    private void Update()
    {
        if (navAgent.remainingDistance < 0.1f)
        {
            currentWaypointIndex = (currentWaypointIndex + 1) % waypoints.Length;
            SetDestinationToWaypoint(currentWaypointIndex);
        }

        // Detect obstacles using raycasting
        if (DetectObstacleAhead())
        {
            // Implement obstacle avoidance logic, such as slowing down or changing lanes.
            // For example, you can adjust the vehicle's speed or path to avoid collisions.
            navAgent.speed = 2.0f; // Reduce speed when an obstacle is detected
        }
        else
        {
            navAgent.speed = 5.0f; // Return to the regular speed
        }
    }

    private void SetDestinationToWaypoint(int index)
    {
        if (index < waypoints.Length)
        {
            navAgent.SetDestination(waypoints[index].position);
        }
    }

    private bool DetectObstacleAhead()
    {
        // Implement raycasting to detect obstacles in front of the agent
        RaycastHit hit;
        if (Physics.Raycast(transform.position, transform.forward, out hit, 5.0f, obstacleLayer))
        {
            Debug.DrawRay(transform.position, transform.forward * hit.distance, Color.red);
            return true;
        }
        else
        {
            Debug.DrawRay(transform.position, transform.forward * 5.0f, Color.green);
            return false;
        }
    }
}
```

3. Set up the Obstacle Layer:

Set the obstacleLayer property in the Inspector of the agent script to the layer(s) you gave to your obstacle objects.

4. Avoidance of Test Obstacles:

Run your scene to see how your agents react to challenges. When obstacles are recognized, they should slow down or take evasive action.

5. Superior Obstacle Avoidance:

You can use advanced obstacle avoidance algorithms such as A* or RVO (Reciprocal Velocity Obstacles) for complex, multi-agent scenarios. Machine learning techniques can also be used to improve obstacle avoidance behaviour.
This basic example lays the groundwork for incorporating obstacle avoidance into your autonomous car agents. Depending on the complexity of your project, you can build on this to construct more sophisticated obstacle avoidance behaviors and decision-making processes.

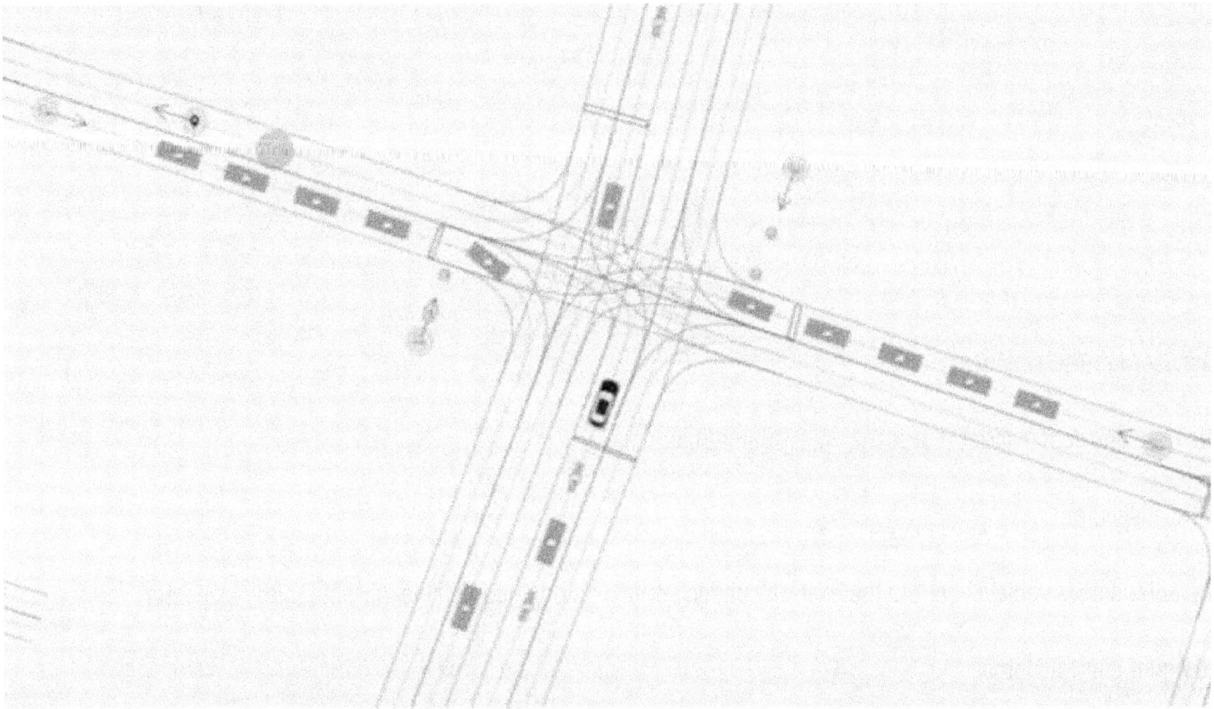

When you add user interaction to your Unity autonomous car simulation, you can control or watch the agents for testing, debugging, and simulation reasons. Using keyboard input as an example, we'll develop a simple user interface (UI) to control an autonomous vehicle in this guide.

1. Design the User Interface (UI):

Create a UI in Unity that includes controls for interacting with your autonomous car. For operations such as accelerating, braking, and steering, you can build UI buttons or sliders.

2. UI Canvas Configuration:

If you haven't previously, make a UI canvas in Unity by right-clicking on the Hierarchy panel and selecting "UI" > "Canvas."

3. Include UI Elements:

Create UI elements like as buttons, sliders, and other UI components to control the vehicle within the canvas. Put these pieces on the screen where you want them.

4. Script for User Interaction:

Make a C# script to manage user interaction with the self-driving vehicle. A simplified example of how to write a basic user interaction script follows:

```
using UnityEngine;

public class UserInteraction : MonoBehaviour
{
    public AutonomousVehicleAgent autonomousVehicle; // Attach the vehicle agent to this variable in the Inspector.

    private void Update()
    {
        // Example: Keyboard input for controlling the vehicle.
        float accelerationInput = Input.GetKey(KeyCode.W) ? 1.0f : 0.0f;
        float brakingInput = Input.GetKey(KeyCode.S) ? 1.0f : 0.0f;
        float steeringInput = Input.GetAxis("Horizontal");

        // Apply user input to control the vehicle.
        autonomousVehicle.ControlVehicle(accelerationInput, brakingInput, steeringInput);
    }
}
```

5. Assign a User Interaction Agent:

Attach the UserInteraction script to a scene empty GameObject.

6. Set up the Inspector:

Attach the autonomous vehicle agent to the UserInteraction script's autonomousVehicle variable in the Inspector.

7. Use the Agent Control Method:

Include a way for controlling the car in your vehicle agent script. This method should accept user input and apply it to the actions of the agent (acceleration, braking, and steering).

8. Experiment and interact:

Run your scenario and control the truck using the keyboard or UI buttons. Observe its behavior and make necessary modifications.

You can construct more elaborate control schemes, employ external input devices, or implement user interfaces for modifying various parameters and analyzing the agent's perception and decision-making for more advanced user involvement.

This simple example allows people to interact with your autonomous vehicle in Unity. Depending on the complexity of your project, you can develop a more complicated user interface, incorporate additional input devices, or employ bespoke control schemes to efficiently test and observe your agents.

AI decision-making is a critical component of creating autonomous vehicle agents that can navigate complex environments and respond to changing conditions. In Unity, you can implement AI decision-making using techniques such as behavior trees, finite state machines, or machine learning. Here, I'll provide a basic example using a finite state machine to control the behavior of your autonomous vehicle agents.

1. State Definition:

Determine which important states your autonomous car agents should exhibit. "FollowPath," "StopAtRedLight," "ObstacleAvoidance," and other states are examples.

2. Construct a Finite State Machine (FSM):

For your finite state machine, write a C# script. A basic example follows:

```
using UnityEngine;

public class FiniteStateMachine : MonoBehaviour
{
    public enum VehicleState { FollowPath, StopAtRedLight, ObstacleAvoidance, CustomState1, CustomState2 }

    private VehicleState currentState;

    private void Start()
    {
        // Initialize the state to the default state.
        currentState = VehicleState.FollowPath;
    }

    private void Update()
    {
        // Implement state transitions and behavior based on the current state.
        switch (currentState)
        {
            case VehicleState.FollowPath:
                // Implement behavior for following the path.
                // You can use the waypoint-based navigation logic from previous steps here.
                break;

            case VehicleState.StopAtRedLight:
                // Implement behavior for stopping at red lights.
                // You can use the traffic light adherence logic from previous steps here.
                break;

            case VehicleState.ObstacleAvoidance:
                // Implement behavior for avoiding obstacles.
                // You can use the obstacle avoidance logic from previous steps here.
                break;

            case VehicleState.CustomState1:
                // Implement behavior for a custom state if needed.
                break;

            case VehicleState.CustomState2:
                // Implement behavior for another custom state if needed.
                break;

                // Add more states and their corresponding behaviors as necessary.
        }
    }

    // Method to change the vehicle's current state.
    public void ChangeState(VehicleState newState)
    {
        currentState = newState;
    }
}
```

3. Include the FSM Script:

In the Unity Inspector, add the FiniteStateMachine script to your autonomous car agent's GameObject.

4. Carry out State Transitions:

Implement logic in your autonomous vehicle agent script to change the current state based on sensory inputs, objectives, and decision-making criteria. For example, sensor data can be used to determine when to switch from "FollowPath" to "ObstacleAvoidance" mode.

5. Test and Observe:

Run your scene and watch how the vehicle agents react based on their present status.

6. Advanced Decision-Making:

You can use behavior trees or machine learning models to make decisions based on complicated inputs and objectives for more advanced AI decision-making. Integrating reinforcement learning libraries, such as Unity's ML-Agents, can enable more sophisticated decision-making.

7. Constantly Refine Behavior:

Adjust state transition criteria, optimize actions, and fine-tune the AI decision-making process based on your project's objectives and needs to continuously develop the agent's behavior.
This simple finite state machine example serves as a foundation for AI decision-making. Depending on the complexity of your project, you can build on this base to develop more complicated decision-making processes and behaviors for your autonomous vehicle agents.

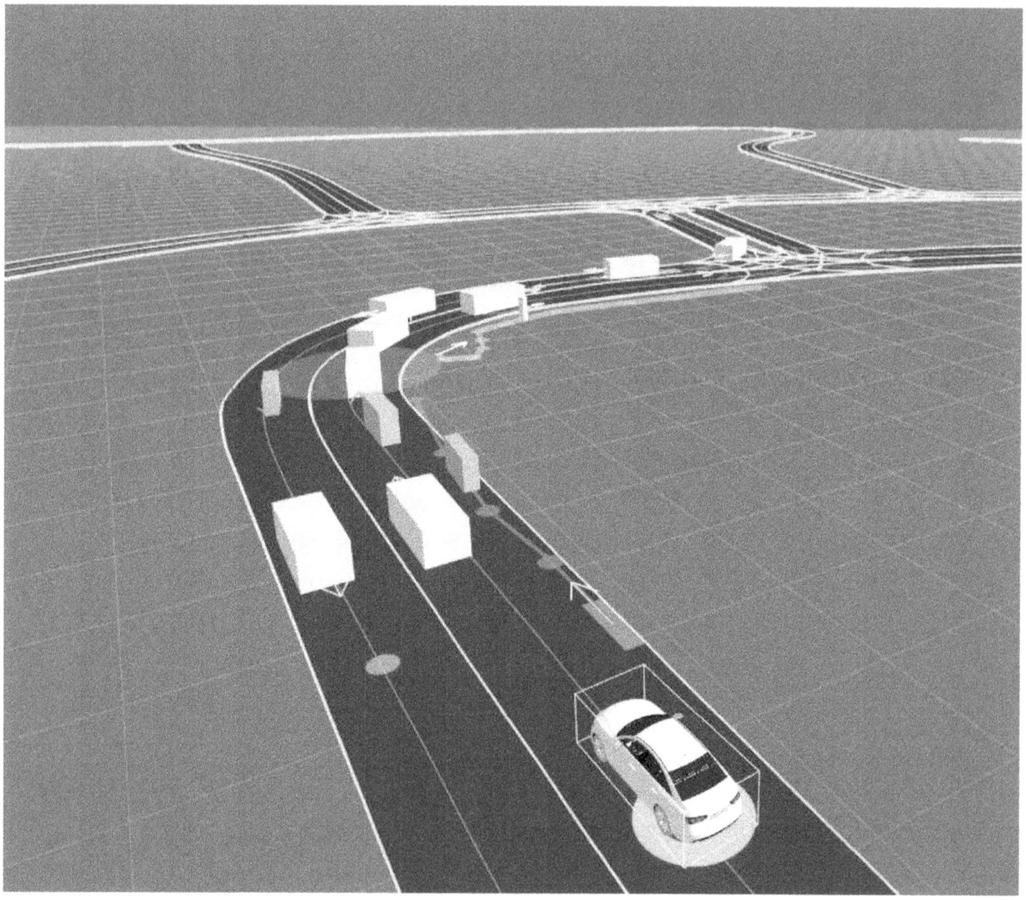

When working with complex simulations such as autonomous car scenarios, performance enhancement in Unity entails refining your project to guarantee it runs efficiently and smoothly. Here are some common suggestions and approaches to help your Unity project run faster:

1. Detail Level (LOD):

Implement LOD models for your scene's objects. As objects move away from the camera, LOD models reduce the degree of information, which can dramatically increase rendering efficiency.

2. Culling:

Reduce the rendering load by using occlusion and frustum culling. The built-in culling mechanisms in Unity can prevent non-visible items from being drawn.

3. Batching:

Combine and batch meshes where possible to reduce draw calls. Dynamic batching can help in some cases, but static batching is more efficient.

4. Texture Compression:

Compress textures to save memory. Texture atlases can be used to combine many textures into a single texture, minimizing draw calls.

5. Quality Preferences:

To match the capabilities of your target platform, adjust the quality settings in your Unity project. For development, use lower quality settings and increase them for final builds.

6. Physics Optimization:

Tune the physics settings, such as collision detection accuracy, to optimize the performance of your physics simulations.

7. Script Optimization:

To find bottlenecks, profile your scripts using Unity's built-in profiler. Reduce needless calculations and memory allocations in your code to optimize it.

8. Asynchronous Loading:

Use asynchronous scene and asset loading to load resources in the background and avoid frame rate drops.

9. Occlusion Queries:

Implement occlusion queries to check whether an object is visible before rendering it. This can be particularly useful for complex scenes.

10. Multithreading:

When possible, use multithreading, especially for CPU-intensive operations. Unity's Job System and Burst Compiler can be of use in this area.

11. GPU Instantiation:

Enable GPU instancing for objects with the same material and characteristics to decrease draw calls and take advantage of parallel processing on the GPU.

12. Audio Enhancement:

Reduce the amount of audio sources and use audio occlusion and attenuation techniques to optimize audio.

13. Streaming Assets:

Stream assets such as textures and models as needed, rather than loading them all at once.

14. GPU Profiling:

Use GPU profiling to identify performance bottlenecks related to rendering. This can help you optimize shaders and rendering processes.

15. Memory Control:

Manage memory more effectively by clearing away things and resources that are no longer in use. To avoid frame rate reductions, use Unity's garbage collector with caution.

16. Level of Detail for Autonomous Vehicles:

Set the degree of detail for autonomous vehicle models and other assets to reduce their complexity at a distance and improve rendering efficiency.

17. Unity Employment System:

Use Unity's Jobs System for multi-threading and parallel processing to improve performance for compute-intensive jobs.

18. Tools for Profiling and Optimization:

Use Unity's profiling and optimization tools to detect and address performance bottlenecks.
Keep in mind that performance improvement is a continuous effort. Maintain a seamless user experience by profiling and monitoring your project's performance on a regular basis, especially in the context of sophisticated simulations like autonomous vehicles.

Here are some additional sophisticated tips for building AI in Unity, particularly for autonomous vehicles or complex simulations:

1. Reinforcement Learning with Machine Learning Agents:

Consider using Unity's ML-Agents toolkit for reinforcement learning if you're constructing autonomous vehicle agents. Through trial and error, you can train agents to make smarter judgments, which can lead to more adaptive behaviors.

2. Personalized Machine Learning Models:

External machine learning libraries, such as TensorFlow or PyTorch, can be used to develop custom machine learning models for advanced AI. You'll have greater say on the architecture and training.

3. Perception with Sensor Fusion:

To construct a more comprehensive perception system, use sensor fusion to incorporate data from numerous sensors (e.g., cameras, LiDAR, radar). Machine learning approaches like sensor fusion neural networks can help with this.

4. Path Planning Algorithms:
For more complex navigation scenarios, use advanced path planning algorithms such as A*, RRT*, or rapidly exploring random trees (RRT). In dynamic situations, these algorithms can determine optimal pathways.

5. Simulation of Traffic:

Using AI-driven non-player cars and pedestrians, create a realistic traffic simulation scene. Advanced traffic simulation can let you evaluate your autonomous vehicles' reactivity in complicated conditions.

6. Deep Reinforcement Learning (DRL):

Implement deep reinforcement learning algorithms, such as Deep Q-Networks (DQN) or Proximal Policy Optimization (PPO), for training autonomous vehicle agents to handle complex scenarios. DRL can lead to more advanced decision-making.

7. Data-Driven Approaches:

Gather and analyze real-world data to train and test your autonomous car agents. To make use of this data, use approaches such as imitation learning or behavioral cloning.

8. Traffic Flow Modeling:

Realistic traffic flows, congestion, and traffic dynamics are modeled. To simulate sophisticated traffic scenarios, consider using traffic simulation tools or developing your own models.

9. Multimodal AI:

Implement multimodal AI systems that can process and fuse data from different sensor types (e.g., images, LiDAR, radar) for enhanced perception and decision-making.

10. Procedural Generation:

Create huge, diverse, and complicated virtual environments for testing and training using procedural generation techniques. Procedural generation can assist you in increasing the complexity of your simulations.

11. Advanced Sensor Models:

Create increasingly sophisticated sensor models, such as physics-based models for LiDAR, radar, and camera sensors. These models can produce realistic sensor data for training and testing.

12. Traffic Management Systems:

To test and challenge your autonomous vehicles, use complex traffic control systems to simulate realistic traffic light timings, road infrastructure, and road behavior.

13. Vehicle Dynamics Simulation:

For a more authentic driving experience, create more realistic vehicle dynamics and physics simulations that take into account tire grip, suspension, and aerodynamics.

14. Advanced Rendering Methods:

Improve the visual quality and realism of your simulation by using advanced rendering techniques such as ray tracing or screen-space reflections.

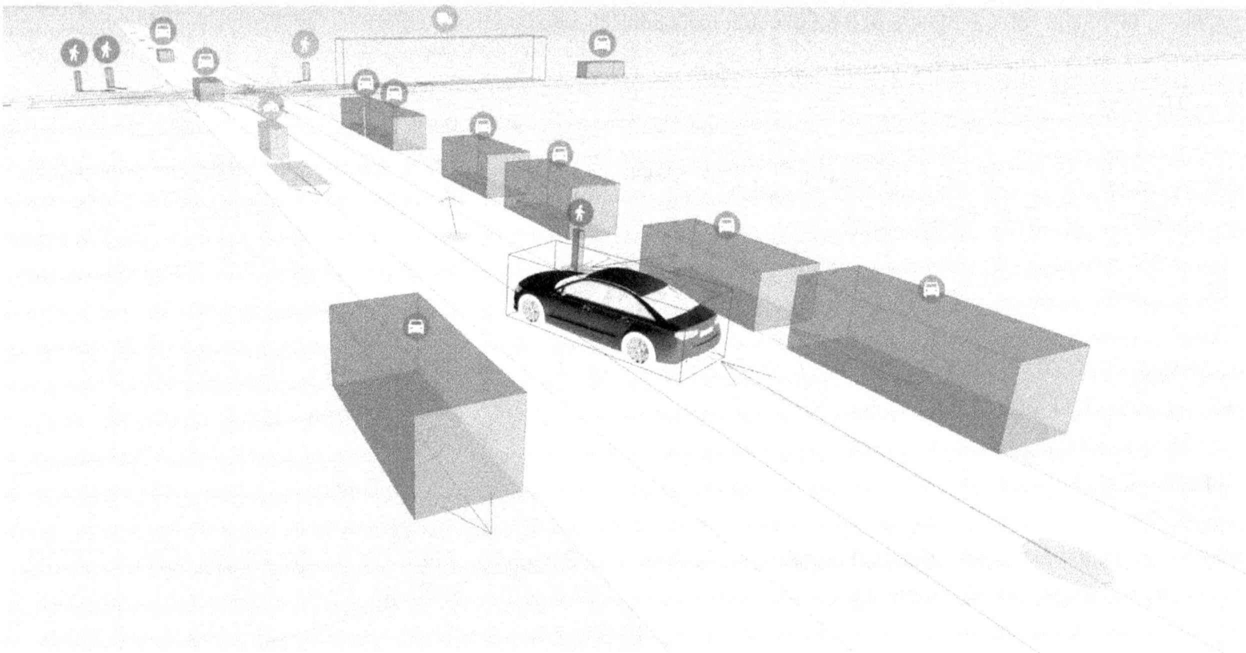

Using advanced AI algorithms in Unity can result in more realistic and resilient autonomous vehicle simulations. Remember that adopting these methodologies may necessitate more advanced knowledge of AI, machine learning, simulation, and Unity development.

References

Chapter I - Noise in Video Games

- Perlin Noise: Ken Perlin's original paper "An Image Synthesizer" (1985)
- Unity Documentation: Unity's built-in Perlin noise functions
- "Texturing & Modeling: A Procedural Approach" by David S. Ebert
- GPU Gems series - Multiple chapters on noise algorithms
- Sebastian Lague's YouTube series on procedural generation

Chapter II - DOTS (Data-Oriented Technology Stack)

- Unity DOTS Documentation - Official Unity ECS manual
- "Data-Oriented Design" by Richard Fabian
- Unity Job System Documentation
- Burst Compiler Documentation
- Mike Acton's CppCon talks on data-oriented design
- Unity's ECS samples repository on GitHub

Chapter III - Editor Scripting

- Unity Scripting API Documentation - EditorWindow, PropertyDrawer classes
- "Unity in Action" by Joe Hocking - Editor scripting chapters
- Unity Manual: Extending the Editor section
- Custom Property Drawers documentation
- ScriptableObject documentation for tool creation

Chapter IV - Scripting Patterns

- "Game Programming Patterns" by Robert Nystrom
- "Design Patterns: Elements of Reusable Object-Oriented Software" (Gang of Four)
- Unity Manual: Best practices for scripting
- "Clean Code" by Robert C. Martin
- Unity's coding standards documentation

Chapter V - Physics System

- Unity Physics Documentation - Rigidbody, Colliders, Joints
- "Real-Time Physics" by Christer Ericson

- Box2D documentation (for 2D physics concepts)
- "Game Physics Engine Development" by Ian Millington
- Unity Physics package documentation (for DOTS physics)

Chapter VI - Shader Programming

- "Real-Time Rendering" by Tomas Akenine-Möller
- Unity Shader Documentation - ShaderLab, HLSL
- "GPU Gems" series (1, 2, and 3)
- Catlike Coding's Unity tutorials - Excellent shader tutorials
- "The Book of Shaders" by Patricio Gonzalez Vivo
- Unity URP/HDRP shader documentation

Chapter VII - AI

- "Artificial Intelligence for Games" by Ian Millington and John Funge
- Unity NavMesh documentation
- "Programming Game AI by Example" by Mat Buckland
- "Behavioral Mathematics for Game AI" by Dave Mark
- Unity ML-Agents documentation for machine learning
- "AI for Game Developers" by David M. Bourg and Glenn Seemann

www.ingramcontent.com/pod-product-compliance
Lightning Source LLC
LaVergne TN
LVHW060043210926
848481LV00013B/3939
* 9 7 9 8 2 3 1 1 2 3 8 8 9 *